It was the custom of my daughter's school to send home occasional notes which the parents had to sign and return. This was to confirm that the notes had been duly read. These notes were often a source of embarrassment to my poor daughter when, in addition to her father's signature, on return they also bore in red ink several corrections to the school's grammar and punctuation. This book is accordingly dedicated to teachers everywhere.

Central bankers like to use enigmatic language. Alan Greenspan, the former chairman of the United States Federal Reserve Board, is probably the world's best known central banker.

His wife is the NBC network's political correspondent, Andrea Mitchell. She once said on radio that Dr Greenspan was characteristically incoherent even when proposing marriage.

Greenspan had to ask for her hand three times before the exact nature of his proposal finally became clear to her.

About the Author

Nick Renton is a consulting actuary, commercial arbitrator, company director and writer. He was born in 1931 and qualified as a Fellow of the Faculty of Actuaries in 1957. He is also a Fellow of the Institute of Actuaries of Australia.

In 1975 he was elected a Fellow of the Securities Institute of Australia for his services to the industry.

After 15 years as Principal Officer of a life insurance company he became the first Executive Director of the Life Offices' Association of Australia from 1975 to 1979. He was Executive Director of the Life Insurance Federation of Australia from its formation in 1979 until 1986. In those capacities he acted as the official spokesman for the life insurance industry.

He is now an independent business consultant to leading stockbrokers, insurance companies, employer organisations, government agencies and others. He also serves on the boards of several financial institutions and is in great demand as a speaker at seminars and conferences.

He was the founder and first president of the Australian Shareholders' Association and has been Federal president of the Australian Society of Security Analysts and Victorian chairman of the Commercial Law Association of Australia.

Nick Renton has been published by 11 different publishers in Australia and the United States. He has written books about more different topics than any other Australian author.

His *Guide for Meetings and Organisations* , published by the Law Book Company, has been widely used as a reference work on all aspects of chairmanship and the running of voluntary associations since it first appeared in 1961. It deals with many practical aspects of meetings procedure not covered in Joske and is now in a two volume seventh edition.

He is also the author of popular books on shares, property, managed investments, taxation, wills, good writing, public relations, the Internet and the Australian economy, as well as of numerous papers to professional bodies.

He has published well over 500 articles in newspapers and financial journals in the last ten or so years.

In 1992 he was awarded the prestigious H M Jackson Memorial Prize for two of his works, *Understanding Dividend Imputation* and the *Retirement Handbook.*

In 1995 he received the Ken Millar Award for his best-selling *Understanding the Stock Exchange* and his highly controversial *Company Directors: Masters or Servants?*

Nick Renton maintains his own web site of over 110 pages at:

http://users.bigpond.net.au/renton

As a free community service this site also invites questions on meetings procedure, family trusts, style and investment terms.

He was made a Member of the Order of Australia in 2004.

He is married and has three children. He lives in Melbourne, Australia.

Some Words About Words

I don't know what "Americanism" means, but it is a damned good word with which to carry an election – A United States senator recontesting his seat

* * *

There is no communication between a writer and a reader who is bored or asleep - anon

* * *

If you stare at any sentence long enough, it will look wrong – Susanna J Sturgis

* * *

When a politician says: "Let me make something perfectly clear", remember that he usually won't – anon

* * *

Television is a medium because it is neither rare nor well done – Ernie Kovacs

* * *

It is not the work of an editor to teach writers how to write - Katherine White

* * *

I write for the same reason I breathe - because if I didn't, I would die - Isaac Asimov

* * *

An editor is a person who knows more about writing than writers do, but has escaped the terrible desire to write – E B White

* * *

A book is only as good as its index – Nick Renton, admonishing one of his publishers

* * *

Read over your compositions and when you meet a passage you think is particularly fine, strike it out - Samuel Johnson

* * *

Don't let a shortcut for the writer become a roadblock for the reader - a plain English expert

* * *

It has been reported that a boy asked his teacher why Jesus Christ was named after a swear word.

* * *

He has never been known to use a word that might send a reader to the dictionary - William Faulkner, about Ernest Hemingway

* * *

Man invented language to satisfy his deep need to complain – Lily Tomlin

* * *

A witty saying proves nothing - Voltaire

* * *

The free flow of information had indeed arrived, but it was the free flow not of an aqueduct but of a sewer - Nick Hudson

* * *

Eschew obfuscation - classical advice to all writers

* * *

First things first! But not necessarily in that order.

* * *

The *Guinness Book of Records* holds the record for being the book most often stolen from public libraries

* * *

"Etc." is a perfect word when you can't think of the right one – E C McKenzie

* * *

Words fascinate me. They always have. For me, browsing in a dictionary is like being turned loose in a bank. - Eddie Cantor

* * *

A book is a gift you can open again and again – Garrison Keillor

* * *

If you can live without writing, then don't do it – Ranier Maria Rilke in*Letter to a Young Poet*

* * *

The United States Supreme Court is the only place where rock music is called intellectual property - anon

* * *

When I use a word it means just what I choose it to mean, neither more nor less – Humpty Dumpty in*Alice in Wonderland* by Lewis Carroll

* * *

Authors of books are merely "letters to the editor" contributors who failed to get their letters published - P G Wodehouse

* * *

All writers need editors, and exceptionally good writers need exceptionally good editors - T S Eliot

* * *

I believe more in the scissors than I do in the pencil – Truman Capote

* * *

Most people think that if something is printed in a book then it must be correct – the author, in the course of a lecture on meetings procedure

* * *

I love deadlines - they make the loveliest whooshing sound as they go by - Douglas Adams

* * *

If someone says: "I know what I mean, but I just can't put it into words", then he doesn't know what he means - anon

* * *

Cats are dangerous companions for writers, because cat watching is a near-perfect method of writing avoidance – Dan Greenburg

* * *

Here lies a can of worms that requires urgent leadership – Jacqui Burke MLA, addressing the ACT Legislative Assembly

* * *

United States Attorney-General John Ashcroft testified before Congress that President Bush is against torture. Yes, he's against torture. Except when it comes to the English language. – David Letterman

* * *

There is no friend as loyal as a book - Ernest Hemingway

* * *

If you take hyphens seriously, you will surely go mad – John Benbow

* * *

Would you convey my compliments to the purist who reads your proofs and tell him that when I split an infinitive, God damn it, I split it so that it will stay split – Raymond Chandler, in a letter to the editor of the*Atlantic Monthly*

* * *

I've always believed in writing without a collaborator, because where two people are writing the same book, each believes he gets all the worry and only half the royalties - Agatha Christie

* * *

Writing became such a process of discovery that I couldn't wait to get to work in the morning: I wanted to know what I was going to say - Sharon O'Brien

* * *

Books are good enough in their own way, but they are a mighty bloodless substitute for life - Robert Louis Stevenson

* * *

Political language is designed to make lies sound truthful and murder respectable, and to give an appearance of solidity to pure wind - George Orwell

* * *

The communication of the dead is tongued with fire beyond the language of the living – inscription on T S Eliot's memorial in Poets' Corner in Westminster Abbey

* * *

Times are bad. Children no longer obey their parents, and everyone is writing a book. – Marcus Tullius Cicero (106-43 BC)

* * *

Toilet out of order. We regret the inconvenience. – Notice on a Manly ferry in Sydney Harbour

* * *

Give me ambiguity or give me something else - bumper sticker

* * *

Important letters that contain no errors will develop errors in the mail - anon

* * *

Move Hitherward the Entire Assembly of Those Who Are Loyal in their Belief – a suggested new title for the hymn better known as *Oh Come, All Ye Faithful*

* * *

Thanks to Mr and Mrs Bernard Shaw for countless suggestions of great value and diversity: and for all the present semicolons – T E Lawrence, in the preface to his *Seven Pillars of Wisdom*

* * *

Freedom of the press is limited to those who own one – A J Liebling

* * *

Q: How many indexers does it take to screw in a light bulb?

A: None. Indexers are kept in the dark until the last possible moment and then expected to work miracles.

* * *

Lexicographer: A writer of dictionaries, a harmless drudge - Samuel Johnson

* * *

Two ladies once complimented the said Dr Johnson on his recently published *Dictionary*, lavishing particular praise on the apparent omission of naughty words. "What? My dears!" Johnson exclaimed. "Then you have been looking for them?"

* * *

KIPLING

In 1889, the editor of the San Francisco *Examiner*, having published one article by Rudyard Kipling, declined to accept any more of the author's work.

The reason? "I'm sorry, Mr Kipling," he explained, "but you just don't know how to use the English language. This isn't a kindergarten for amateur writers."

Eight years later, Kipling (who had already written *The Man Who would be King)* was awarded the Nobel Prize for Literature.

* * *

BAFFLEGAB

Milton A Smith, assistant general counsel for the US Chamber of Commerce, has coined the word "bafflegab" for incomprehensible or pretentious language, especially bureaucratic jargon.

When asked to briefly define his word, Smith replied:

"Multiloquence characterised by consummate interfusion of circumlocution or periphrasis, inscrutability, and other familiar manifestations of abstruse expatiation commonly utilised for promulgations implementing procrustean determinations by governmental bodies."

* * *

IN CONCLUSION, A USELESS STATISTIC:

If 99.9 per cent were considered "good enough", then there would be about 25 spelling mistakes in the Australian Concise Oxford Dictionary - Nick Renton

Contents

Foreword

Nick Renton is a person with a passion for language and in particular a great love for the English language. In this, his 60th book, he shares this enthusiasm with his readers, offering them advice, interesting facts and figures, and illustrative anecdotes, much of them in good humour.

The same enthusiasm makes him a guardian of standards, but I am glad I was not his daughter's schoolteacher! In this short Foreword, I will confine myself to the second and third parts of the book, Part I being the area where sociolinguists like me and prescriptivists like him hold diametrically opposed views.

Many of the well-chosen extracts in Parts II and III demonstrate the importance of thinking before you speak or write. Careless formulation can lead to misinterpretation but also to entertainment.

When Nick Renton subjects forms and guidelines to scrutiny, he articulates the frustrations of many a fellow citizen. Through priceless examples from newspaper headlines and from the domains of finance, romance and zoology he enlightens and entertains. My favourite is the punctuation in Gloria's love letter.

Metaphors receive substantial treatment, as do word puzzles. Each chapter is preceded by a witty quotation, and relevant web sites are indicated.

Readers will be provoked into watching their style, into learning, thinking, laughing and agreeing or disagreeing. I wish Nick Renton well on Book 60.

Michael Clyne AM
Professorial Fellow, School of Languages and Linguistics, University of Melbourne

Preface

As a practising writer I have always taken a great interest in the English language. In this new book I have endeavoured to share some of my enthusiasm with other writers, with students and with the many lovers of words. I have also included some interesting linguistic items collected by me over the last fifty or so years.

The book is in three parts. The first part deals with a number of serious issues of relevance to persons who want to improve the quality of their writing. The rest of the book is in a lighter vein.

Part I starts with two chapters dealing with common errors of grammar and spelling. While these chapters are, of course, merely brief executive summaries of what could have been said, they do in fact present material relating to about 90 per cent of today's problem areas.

In order to assist writers to maintain internal consistency in their literary output - a most important ingredient of all good writing - this book is deliberately and unashamedly prescriptive rather than descriptive.

Part II is a real potpourri and deals with a number of unrelated issues which lovers of words will find of interest. The topics discussed include Basic English, metaphors and some curiosities of the English language. One chapter features assorted lists - some useful, others just tongue-in-cheek.

Part III contains three short stories. While lighthearted, each carries a subtle message.

The main text concludes with a Tailpiece - a series of jokes about the English language gathered together over many years. Some of these will, no doubt, also prove useful to readers who are involved in public speaking, especially when they are composing the opening and closing remarks of their presentations.

The work also features an appendix containing useful information.

The book will serve a number of assorted purposes, including those set out below. Apart from entertaining its readers, the book will:

- assist writers and public speakers to become more articulate
- provide resource material for writers, editors and teachers of English
- show students and lovers of words the richness and diversity of the living English language
- help persons for whom English is a second language.

N E Renton AM
http://users.bigpond.net.au/renton
nrenton@bigpond.net.au

PART I

RULES FOR WRITERS IN A NUTSHELL

CHAPTER 1

Common Grammatical Errors

Some guy hit my fender, and I said to him, "Be fruitful and multiply," but not in those words.

- Woody Allen

BACKGROUND

It has been said before, but it bears repeating: standards in many walks of life are slipping.

Most people want to express themselves in correct English, yet numerous different types of error affecting spelling, grammar and punctuation occur in many forms of communication.

Many, although by no means all, spelling errors can be detected by automatic spelling checkers and in case of doubt reference can always be made to a dictionary.

However, the other two types of error are more troublesome - but about 90 per cent of the grammatical and punctuation mistakes being made by speakers and writers today fall into the relatively small number of categories set out below.

Thus persons who wish to become more accurate but who lack the time or the patience to study the subject in depth might find it worth while to note at least the basic items included in the brief summary which follows.

SUMMARY OF THE KEY ISSUES

Confusion (often in both directions) between *homophones*, pairs of words which look and/or sound somewhat similar:

their	there
principal	principle
stationary	stationery
complement	compliment
complementary	complimentary
affect	effect
licence (noun)	license (verb)
practice (noun)	practise (verb)
led (past)	lead (present)
misled (past)	mislead (present)
foreword	forward
personnel	personal
infer	imply
elicit	illicit
discrete	discreet
formally	formerly
loath	loathe
born	borne

To illustrate: *The warnings had lead him to stop smoking.* This should be "led".

In some cases more than two words can be involved - for example: *site*, *sight* and *cite.*

Words not rendered correctly:

Incorrect Form	**Correct Form**
a criteria	a criterion (singular)
a criteria	criteria (plural)
a phenomena	a phenomenon (singular)

Incorrect Form	Correct Form
a phenomena	phenomena (plural)
like	such as
recieve	receive
hung (in relation to persons)	hanged
gender (in relation to persons)	sex
alright	all right
in arrears	in arrear (cf. in advance)
mortgagor	mortgagee (the lender)
mortgagee	mortgagor (the borrower)
power of attorney (a document)	attorney under power (the person)
Lady and Gentlemen (form of address at a meeting)	Madam and Gentlemen
disinterested (as the opposite of "interested")	uninterested

Incorrect use of metric symbols - for example:

> *kms* or even *kmls* instead of *km* for *kilometres*
>
> *kmh* or *kph* instead of *km/h* for *kilometres per hour*

Incorrect use of the nominative case, of which typical examples are:

> *Who do you call?* instead of *Whom do you call?*
>
> *To treat we Australians in this way is wrong.* instead of *To treat us Australians in this way is wrong.*
>
> *This is strictly between you and I.* instead of *This is strictly between you and me.*

Incorrect use of the accusative case, of which typical examples are:

> *Whom shall I say is calling?* instead of *Who shall I say is calling?* as is obvious if the parenthetical words are omitted: *Who ... is calling?*
>
> *We make the decisions, not them.* instead of *We make the decisions, not they.* Nobody would want to say "them make the decisions".
>
> *He spoke to a woman whom he knew was a reporter.* instead of *He spoke to a woman who he knew was a reporter.* Again, consider "a woman who ... was a reporter".
>
> *The delay was due to him going on holidays.* instead of *The delay was due to his going on holidays.* The cause was the "going on holidays", not the person.

Incorrect duplication of "that" - for example:

> *We know that subject to one item that we can proceed.* instead of *We know that subject to one item we can proceed.*

Incorrect positioning of "both" - for example:

> *It was signed both by John and Mary.* instead of *It was signed by both John and Mary.*

Misplacements of "only" so that it modifies the wrong word - for example:

> *This is only available to adults.* instead of *This is available only to adults.*

The pronoun "they" used with a singular antecedent - for example:

> *Nobody felt that they were responsible.* instead of *Nobody felt that he was responsible.* or *No persons felt that they were responsible.*

Incorrect form of the verb - for example:

> *It has and continues to cause trouble.* instead of *It has caused and continues to cause trouble.*

Incorrect negative or interrogative forms of the verb "used to" - for example:

> *She did not use to gamble.* instead of *She used not to gamble.*

The use of "that" instead of "as" after "same" or "such" - for example:

> *This is the same book that I had read.* instead of *This is the same book as I had read.*

PUNCTUATION

Incorrect use of commas with relative clauses, in both directions - for example:

> Defining relative clauses: *Books, which are in Japanese, cannot be read by most Australians.* instead of *Books which are in Japanese cannot be read by most Australians.* (Here the words starting with "which" are essential to the meaning of "books" and thus should not be separated by commas.) Alternatively, this sentence could be rendered as *Books that are in Japanese cannot be read by most Australians.* Some writers prefer "that" to "which" in such constructions.
>
> Non-defining relative clauses: *Books which are more expensive than newspapers are nonetheless widely read by Australians.* instead of *Books, which are more expensive than newspapers, are nonetheless widely read by Australians.* (Here the words starting with "which" are purely for additional information and are not essential to the meaning of "books". They should thus appear between commas.) In this structure "which" cannot be replaced by "that".

Illogical commas between subject and verb, destroying the flow of the message - for example:

> *The sample of about 7500 tonnes, is to be shipped in October.*

Incorrect placement of closing brackets adjacent to full stops, in both directions - for example:

> *Poor people pay too much tax (at least in Australia.)* instead of *Poor people pay too much tax (at least in Australia).*
>
> *Poor people pay too much tax. (This is a problem in Australia).* instead of *Poor people pay too much tax. (This is a problem in Australia.)*

Apostrophes omitted where required - for example:

> *The books cover was the wrong colour.* instead of *The book's cover was the wrong colour.*
>
> *Is this our countries best effort?* instead of *Is this our country's best effort?*

Apostrophes used where not required (especially for ordinary plurals) - for example:

> *These dictionary's are your's.* instead of *These dictionaries are yours.*

This error is particularly common for nouns such as "photo's". It is often referred to as the "greengrocer's apostrophe" because of the prevalence of signs such as "cheap pear's".

The use of the apostrophe for pronouns is discussed in Chapter 2.

Apostrophes inserted in the wrong place - for example:

> *The woman juror's room is around the corner.* instead of *The woman jurors' room is around the corner.*

Poor punctuation can even reverse meanings. Compare these two advertising slogans:

> Smith and Son: We're Number One for Car Repairs
>
> Smith and Son Were Number One for Car Repairs

See also Chapter 15.

OTHER ASPECTS

There is also a common oral error - referring to the letter *H* as "haitch" instead of as "aitch".

Two other common problem areas need special mention:

- the limitations of spelling checkers and the failure to use one even if it is available
- the failure to be internally consistent.

The words "its" and "it's" and similar terms are discussed in Chapter 2.

Some other particularly troublesome words are discussed in Chapter 3; these include "disinterested", "principal", "principle", "affect", "effect" and "like".

Finally, a curiosity. Google reports about 70,000 instances of "let he" when the correct usage would be "let him". Many of these are mistranslations of the well-known biblical passage in John 8:7 (Jesus: "He that is without sin among you, let him first cast a stone at her" in the King James Version, sometimes rendered more simply as "let him who is without sin cast the first stone").

CHAPTER 2

Common Spelling Errors

A migrant who had tried very hard to master the intricacies of the English language shot himself. He had just read a placard outside a theatre. It had said: "Noel Coward's 'Cavalcade': Pronounced Success."

BACKGROUND

Despite the ready availability of spelling checkers instances of incorrect renderings abound. To illustrate, at the time of writing:

- Google is reporting a staggering 1.13 million instances of the word "recieve" on the Internet.
- The web site of the Department of Health and Ageing, the Australian government department charged with handling accommodation bonds, frequently misspells that key word as "accomodation".

This chapter lists:

- Words which are frequently misspelt.
- Commonly used words which can be spelt in more than one way, showing the preferred version first and other versions in {curly brackets}.

- Words the correct spelling of which tends to be controversial, with comments on the issues.
- Some words which require capitals or which might be thought of as requiring capitals.
- Some expressions best written as one word rather than two, or vice versa.

ALPHABETICAL LIST

a to z

abridgement {abridgment}

accommodate

accommodation

Achilles' heel

acknowledgement {acknowledgment}

acreage

actuarial

actuary

adaptation. Not "adaption".

admissible

advice (noun), advise (verb)

adviser {advisor}

ageing

aitch. the letter H. The word is not "haitch", as commonly thought. The word is derived from the Latin *ahha* and the expected "h" symbol for the name of the letter is thus actually to be found in a disguised form at the end of the word "aitch".

all right. Not "alright"; not to be confused with the form used for "already".

anyone. Not "any one".

Anzac

appreciable

arm's length
assessable
awkward
back door (noun), backdoor (adjective)
barbecue
bachelor
benefited
benefiting
biased
blond (male), blonde (female)
bookkeeper. Not "book-keeper".
bookkeeping. Not "book-keeping".
bureaux
bushfire
byelection {by-election}
bylaw {by-law}
calendar
cannot. Not "can not".
capsize. Not "capsise"; "-ize" is not a suffix here.
Celsius. Not "Celcius".
census
chargeable
cipher
clear-cut
coat of arms
colour {color}
common sense (noun), commonsense (adjective)
comparative
concede
connection. Not "connexion".
consensus. Not "concensus".

convenor {convener}

copyright. Not "copywrite".

Corporations Act (no apostrophe)

deductible

dependant (noun), dependent (adjective). Contrast "independent" (noun and adjective).

depreciable

dextrous {dexterous}

dietitian {dietician}

dilemma

disastrous

disc, disk. The words "disk" and "diskette" are computer terms; in other contexts "disc" is normal.

disfranchise. Not "disenfranchise".

dispatch {despatch}

dissociate. Not "disassociate".

downside. Not "down side".

dyke

e-mail

each other

embarrass

endorse {indorse}

enquire, enquiry. See "inquire", "inquiry".

enrol

enrolled

enrolling

extraordinary. Not "extra ordinary".

facsimile. But the abbreviation is "fax".

focused {focussed}

focusing {focussing}

foetal

foetus

for ever {forever}

foreword. Not “forward” when referring to an introduction to a book, nor “foreward”.

forgather

fulfil

fulfilled

fulfilling

fulfilment

gaol. The American-sounding “jail” is more logical, although “gaol” continues in official use in Australia.

gauge

goodwill. Not “good will”.

gram

grateful

grey {gray}

guarantee. Not “guaranty”.

haemorrhage

harass

harbour {harbor}

holistic. Not “wholistic”.

home page

honorarium

honorary

honorific

honour

honourable

however

humorist

immerse

immovable

in so far

inasmuch

inbetween {in between}

independent (noun and adjective). Contrast "dependant" (noun), "dependent" (adjective).

indorse. See "endorse".

input taxed (not hyphenated, as it is a statutory term)

inquire {enquire}, inquiry {enquiry}

Internet

intranet

Iraqi. Not "Iraqui".

jackeroo

jail {gaol}

judgement {judgment}

keyword

labour

largesse {largess}

liaise, liaison

licence (noun), license (verb)

licensee

likeable {likable}

linchpin

liquorice

lodgement {lodgment}

manoeuvre

manufactures, chamber of. Not "manufacturers" in this context.

maybe (adverb). Not "may be".

memento

meter (an instrument for measuring things), metre (a unit of length, 1000 mm)

mileage {milage}

mistakenly. Not "mistakingly".

moneyed

movable

Muslim {Moslem}

net {nett}

nevertheless. Not "never the less" or "never-the-less".

next of kin

no one

nonetheless. Not "none the less" or "none-the-less".

notwithstanding

office-bearer

offices. Not "officers" in "life offices".

offline

omelette

ongoing

online

outmanoeuvre

overdo

parallel

paid. Not "payed".

payroll. Not "pay-roll" except when quoting Acts of Parliament using that spelling.

per cent (two words, no full stop). Not "per centum". The symbol "%" can be used in tables, but preferably not in text.

percentage (one word). Not "%age".

permissible

phoney

playwright. Not "playwrite".

policymaker. Not "policy maker" or "policy-maker".

practice (noun), practise (verb)

precede (compare "secede"; contrast "proceed", "succeed")

preventive {preventative}

privilege

proceed (compare "succeed"; contrast "precede", "secede")

program {programme} (in all senses)

publicly. Not "publically".

pyjamas

qango. Acronym for "quasi-autonomous national government organisation". Not "quango".

rateable {ratable}

ratepayer. Not "rate payer".

rebateable {rebatable}

receive. Not "recieve".

receptionist

relief

renounceable

rescind, rescission

restaurateur. Not "restauranteur".

saleable {salable}

saveable {savable}

scapegoat. Not "scrapegoat"; the word is connected with "escape".

sceptic

sceptical

Scots (or "Scottish"). Not "Scotch", except in relation to whisky.

secede (compare "precede"; contrast "proceed", "succeed")

seize

sizeable {sizable}

skilful

smorgasbord. Not "smorgasboard".

somesuch (demonstrative pronoun), some such (two adjectives) sound bite

strait (noun)

subheading

subsidiary

succeed (compare "proceed"; contrast "precede", "secede")

succinct

suchlike

supersede

swap {swop}

T-shirt. Not "tee-shirt".

taxpayer. Not "tax payer".

tenant. Not "tennant".

thank you. Not "thankyou".

themselves. Not "themself".

threshold. Contrast "withhold".

tradeable {tradable}

typist

under way

unlikeable {unlikable}

unparalleled

unsaleable {unsalable}

upside. Not "up side".

usable {useable}

usage

user-friendly

vacuum

veranda

vineyard

vintner

web site

whatever

whenever

wherever

Wiener schnitzel. Not "Weiner"; the word is German for "Viennese".

withhold. Contrast "threshold".

world wide web

worth while (preposition plus noun), worthwhile (adjective). The noun is used in phrases such as "to be worth while", which is short for "to be worth somebody's while".

worldwide

yield. Not "yeild".

Yours faithfully. Not "Your's".

Yours sincerely. Not "Your's".

Yours truly. Not "Your's".

COMPOUND WORDS

Compound words are often found in up to three different versions - for example:

- *asset holder* (two separate words)
- *asset-holder* (one hyphenated word)
- *assetholder* (one unhyphenated word).

In most cases there is no single "correct" version, but, as in all other areas of writing, consistency in regard to any particular term within the confines of a single piece of writing is essential.

It is suggested that, generally speaking, expressions involving *holder* in regard to persons should be rendered as a single unhyphenated word - for example:

bondholder

cardholder

debentureholder

keyholder
landholder
leaseholder
noteholder
officeholder
optionholder
policyholder
proxyholder
shareholder
stakeholder
unitholder

However, in some cases two words seem better - for example:

account holder
asset holder
licence holder
passport holder
patent holder

On the other hand, in reference to objects being *held* two words are always appropriate - for example:

cup holder
napkin holder
pencil holder
toothpick holder

POSSESSIVE PRONOUNS AND ADJECTIVES

The absence of apostrophes in the case of certain possessive pronouns often seems to lead to spelling mistakes. The following table sets out the position:

Personal or Relative Pronoun	Correct Possessive Pronoun	Incorrect Possessive Pronouns Commonly Used	Possessive Adjective
she	hers	her's	her
it	its	it's, its'	its
we	ours	our's	our
you	yours	your's	your
they	theirs	their's	their
who	whose	who's	whose

This book is mine, but that one is hers. Whose pen is that?

There is also confusion (in both directions) between certain pairs:

- The correct possessive adjective corresponding to "it" is "its", not "it's" (which is short for "it is").
- The correct possessive adjective corresponding to "you" is "your", not "you're" (which is short for "you are").
- The correct possessive adjective corresponding to "they" is "their", not "they're" (which is short for "they are") or "there".
- The correct possessive adjective corresponding to "who" is "whose", not "who's" (which is short for "who is").

It's raining. Who's coming to dinner?

In some cases "it's" can also be short for "it has" and "who's" for "who has":

It's been a long day. Who's received a parcel?

-ISE VERSUS -IZE

Although the suffixes "-ize" for verbs and "-ization" for the corresponding nouns are normally used in the United States the forms "-ise" and "-isation" are recommended for use in Australia

- for example, *organise, organisation.* However, there are four exceptions:

capsize

prize

seize

size

There are a number of words which always need to be spelt using "-ise", whatever form is used for the rest:

advertise

advise

apprise

arise

chastise

circumcise

comprise

compromise

demise

despise

devise

disfranchise

disguise

enfranchise

enterprise

excise

exercise

franchise

improvise

incise

merchandise

poise

praise

premise
promise
raise
revise
rise
supervise
surmise
surprise
televise

SPELLING AND GRAMMAR

It is reported that Peter Sellers, while appearing on the *Goon Show*, received a curious letter from one of the programme's fans:

> "Dear Mr. Sellers, I have been a keen follower of yours for many years now, and should be most grateful if you would kindly send me a singed *sic* photograph of yourself."

Encouraged by his friend and fellow-comedian Harry Secombe, Sellers carefully burned the edges of one of his publicity photographs with his cigarette lighter - and sent it off by return mail.

Several weeks later, another letter arrived from the same address:

> "Dear Mr. Sellers, Thank you very much for the photograph, but I wonder if I could trouble you for another, as this one is signed *sic* all round the edge."

Many people rely on spelling checkers on their computers to correct their work. They are certainly valuable in catching not only errors from ignorance but also typographical errors including accidentally duplicated words. But they are no help at all when dealing with errors of the kind illustrated in the above anecdote or with mistakes of the *principle/principal there/their* type.

In contrast, grammar checkers, while fine in theory, at this stage of their development are more nuisance than they are worth and are best turned off.

Some common grammar errors are discussed in http://users.bigpond.net.au/renton/930.htm

THE SPELLING CHECKER

The following famous poem illustrates the point made above:

> Eye have a spelling chequer
> It came with my pea see
> It plane lea marques four my revue
> Miss steaks i can knot sea.
>
> Eye strike a quay and type a word
> And weight four it two say
> Weather eye am wrong oar write
> It shows me strait a weigh.
>
> As soon as a mist ache is maid
> It nose bee fore two long
> And eye can put the error rite
> Its rare lea ever wrong.
>
> Aye ran this poem threw it
> I'm shore your pleased two no
> Its letter perfect in it's weigh
> My chequer tolled me sew.
>
> - Sauce unknown

CHAPTER 3

Vocabulary Issues

When General Motors introduced the Chevy Nova in South America, the company was apparently unaware that "no va" means "it won't go" in Spanish.

SOME POPULAR MISCONCEPTIONS

A number of expressions in colloquial use are based on a misunderstanding as to the correct meaning of the literal words.

Some examples of this are as follows:

- "A leading question" (a very pertinent question): This involves the misuse of a legal term used in relation to cross-examinations - a term which actually means a question so framed as to suggest the answer.
- "Opening gambit" (the first in a series of strategic moves): This is a tautological expression, which also involves a misunderstanding of a technical chess term concerned with the making of a sacrifice.
- "To create a Frankenstein" (to create something wicked and out of control): This is a reference to the fictional *creator* of "Frankenstein's monster" in a story by M W Shelley, in mistake for a reference to the monster itself.

- "At the eleventh hour" (at the last moment): As a day has 24 hours and half a day has 12 hours, this phrase is doubly wrong; "at the twenty-fourth hour" would be much more logical. (The phrase actually refers to the twelve hours between sunrise and sunset, the "day" in biblical times, and to the method referred to in Matthew 20:1-16 of paying labourers in a vineyard. These were all paid the same for their work, irrespective of whether they had been working all day or had started only just before the last full hour of the Roman working day, because they first turned up during the eleventh hour.)

The expression "light years" is often used incorrectly to mean "a long time". It is actually a term used in astronomy. A "light year" is the *distance* travelled by light in a twelve months period.

Another common practice is to use the phrase "to come full circle" - which obviously implies returning to one's original starting point - in mistake for another expression, "to turn around 180 degrees" - which means reversing one's previous stance and now going in the opposite direction.

Some other misunderstandings frequently encountered are:

- the use of "litmus test" to mean a selection procedure
- the use of "marching orders" to mean instructions in general
- the use of "to cut the Gordian knot" instead of another expression, namely, "to cut the umbilical cord".

Sometimes the popular meaning of a phrase acquires a different emphasis from that intended by the classical author. For example, "to be an albatross around someone's neck", from Samuel Taylor Coleridge's *The Rime of the Ancient Mariner*, now usually means "to be a great burden from which one cannot easily escape". The original overtones of doom and the earlier meaning of the phrase, "a source of bad luck", rarely apply nowadays.

"To have one's cake and eat it" is illogical; "to eat one's cake and have it" would make much more sense.

In a rather different category is the large hollow wooden horse used by the Greek soldiers in order to enter the ancient city of Troy. It is usually referred to as the "Trojan horse" and the expression in this form is used as a modern metaphor. However, it is obvious that the structure was really a "Greek horse".

To "beg the question" is to commit the logical fallacy of assuming the truth of the very matter in dispute. The phrase does not mean "to raise the question". Neither does it mean to "to avoid the question".

Speakers sometimes say "divide by half" when they really mean "divide by two" or "halve". To "divide by half" is actually the same as to "multiply by two".

The word "literal" itself can be misused - for example, in expressions such as: "It literally made my blood boil."

DISINTERESTED

The word *disinterested* means "impartial or unbiased" and "without any vested interest".

A very common error is to use it when "uninterested" or "lacking in enthusiasm" is really meant.

FLAMMABLE

The words "inflammable" and "flammable" both mean "capable of being set on fire".

The former was the original term, but because the prefix "in-", here meaning "into", gave the dangerously misleading impression of meaning "not", the latter version was coined.

On safety grounds, rather than for linguistic reasons, use of the word "flammable" is accordingly strongly recommended.

VIZ.

As the abbreviation "viz." (for the Latin *videlicet*) is always pronounced "namely" it seems preferable to be less pretentious and to use the actual English word "namely" instead.

Incidentally, both "viz." and "namely" need to be followed by a comma - for example, "namely, speech".

HARDLY

The sentence:

> *There are hardly no apples left.*

should read

> *There are hardly any apples left.*

or possibly

> *There are virtually no apples left.*

In English the temptation to use "no" or "not" to reinforce the negative connotations implicit in the word "hardly" must be resisted, although interestingly enough the corresponding French expression for that word approaches the matter the other way round. The French say *ne ... guère*, effectively *not ... hardly.*

The sentence:

> *Almost hardly any questions were sent in.*

must be rendered as

> *Hardly any questions were sent in.*

or as

> *Almost no questions were sent in.*

Again:

> *He left before you had hardly time to welcome him.*

should be

> *He left almost before you had time to welcome him.*

or

> *You hardly had time to welcome him before he left.*

> *The show can't end before it's hardly begun.*

should be reworded on the lines of

> *The show can't end yet, as it has only just begun.*

> *Surrendering this battle before it's hardly begun is no way to win.*

should be reworded on the lines of

> *Surrendering this battle, which has only just begun, is no way to win.*

> *The ship sank before it was hardly out of the port.*

should be reworded on the lines of

> *The ship was hardly out of the port before it sank.*

PRINCIPAL, PRINCIPLE

As an adjective, "principal" means chief; as a noun, either a chief person (headmaster, proprietor of a business, partner in a firm, star performer, person who appoints an agent, and so on) or the capital sum in a loan transaction.

This word should not to be confused with "principle", a fundamental doctrine.

AFFECT, EFFECT

As a noun "effect" means "result". As a verb "to effect" means "to bring about".

This word should not to be confused with "affect", to have an effect on.

BORN, BORNE

The verb *to bear* has two different past participles, *born* and *borne*, which should not be confused.

The form *borne* is used:

- In contexts unrelated to births - for example: *The cost of this is borne by the tenant* or *The plan has borne fruit.*
- In contexts related to births, in the active voice - for example: *She has borne three children.*
- In contexts related to births, in the passive voice with "by" - for example: *The children borne by her were all male.*

The other form, *born*, is used for meanings such as "brought forth by birth" or "destined from birth to be" something or other - for example: *He was born last Friday* or *She was born to be rich.*

LIKE, SUCH AS

The preposition "like" implies similarity or resemblance, as in "she looks like my sister". It should not be used as a synonym for "such as" or "for example". Thus:

Deductions from certain items like interest may be made.

should read

Deductions from certain items such as interest may be made.

The sentence:

Here we get privileges like they get in Canberra.

should read

Here we get privileges such as those they get in Canberra.

Similarly:

It rained like yesterday.

should be

It rained, as was the case yesterday.

or alternatively

Today, like yesterday, was a rainy day.

FEWER, LESS

The adjective *fewer* refers to numbers - for example, *fewer than 20 items, fewer chances.*

The adjective *less* refers to quantities - for example, *less than 20 metres long, less wealth.*

NICHT WAHR

The English equivalent of the conversational German "nicht wahr?" and the French "n'est-ce pas?" is to turn an affirmative statement into a negative elliptical question and vice versa:

We are late, aren't we?

We did not miss anything, did we?

Buses leave here frequently, don't they?

Expressions such as

He is Swiss, or is he?

and

They get to know each other better every time they speak. Or do they?

are thus not only unidiomatic - they are also illogical in having two *identical* propositions linked by "or" (the conjunction used for alternatives).

MULTIPLE MEANINGS

Does the command *secure this building* mean:

- Defend it by posting armed guards?
- Buy it regardless of price?
- Lock all the doors and windows?

EDUCATION IN THE UK

The British government's Department for Education sent out lots of glossy posters to schools at vast expense to promote its literacy campaign through extending children's vocabulary. Such a pity that they spelt it "vocabluary".

EXAMPLES OF UGLY NEW TERMS

The following new words are amongst those included for the first time in the 355,000-word single-volume *Oxford Dictionary of English* (revised second edition), published on 10 August 2005:

chugger (a collector for a charity who "mugs" his victims by approaching them in the street)

clueful (knowledgeable)

cockapoo (a crossbreed derived from a cocker spaniel and a miniature poodle)

dramedy (a dramatic comedy)

eighty-six (to reject, discard or destroy)

Greek god (an extremely handsome man)

greige (a colour between grey and beige)

leverage (to use something to maximum advantage)

mitumba (second-hand clothing)

picturize (to adapt a story for a film)

snagging (the process of checking a new building for minor faults that need to be rectified) sock hop (a social dance at which participants dance in their stockinged feet)

spendy (expensive)

twofer (two items sold for the price of one)

ABRAHAM LINCOLN'S GETTYSBURG ADDRESS

This is the famous 269-word speech which United States President Abraham Lincoln gave on 9 November 1863 at the dedication of a national cemetery on the field of Gettysburg. It is often quoted as a particularly fine piece of oratory.

Four score and seven years ago our fathers brought forth on this continent a new nation, conceived in liberty and dedicated to the proposition that all men are created equal.

Now we are engaged in a great civil war, testing whether that nation or any nation so conceived and so dedicated can long endure.

We are met on a great battlefield of that war. We have come to dedicate a portion of that field as a final resting place for those who here gave their lives that that nation might live. It is altogether fitting and proper that we should do this. But, in a larger sense, we cannot dedicate, we cannot consecrate, we cannot hallow this ground.

The brave men, living and dead, who struggled here have consecrated it far above our poor power to add or detract. The world will little note nor long remember what we say here, but it can never forget what they did here.

It is for us the living rather to be dedicated here to the unfinished work which they who fought here have thus far so nobly advanced. It is rather for us to be here dedicated to the great task remaining before us - that from these honored dead we take increased devotion to that cause for which they gave the last full measure of devotion; that we here highly resolve that these dead shall not have died in vain; that this nation, under God, shall have a new birth of freedom; and that government of the people, by the people, for the people shall not perish from the earth.

DIFFERENT POINTS OF VIEW

On a lighter note, consider the following:

The president of our organisation is better than the president of their organisation.

Their president is as hard as nails

　　Our president stands firm

Their president never gives up

　　Our president always follows through

Their president is very aggressive

　　Our president is dynamic

Their president is fussy

　　Our president has a good eye for detail

Their president is stuck up

　　Our president is very assured

Their president is stubborn

　　Our president is strong-willed

Their president is pushy

　　Our president argues professionally

Their president acts impulsively

　　Our president makes quick decisions

Their president is obdurate

　　Our president shows determination

Their president connives with cronies

Our president co-operates with colleagues

Their president is pig-headed

Our president knows his mind

Their president is obstinate

Our president is self-assertive

Their president is inflexible

Our president is resolute

Their president is intractable

Our president shows admirable persistence

Their president manipulates people

Our president makes good use of the available talent

Their president wields undue influence

Our president commands universal respect

Their president likes to hatch plots

Our president is a good lateral thinker

Their president has fanciful ideas

Our president is a great visionary

Their president conspires with a clique

Our president plans with a sound team

Their president is slow

Our president is thorough

Their president is a would-be clever person

Our president shows initiative

Their president is conceited

Our president is self-confident

Their president jumps on every bandwagon

Our president is receptive to good ideas

Their president likes to drop names

Our president is willing to share his contacts

Their president spreads propaganda

Our president does a marvellous PR job

CHAPTER 4

Gobbledegook

We tried to set an example
of clear, straightforward language, free
from technical jargon

- Sir Robert Garran, Secretary of the
Attorney-General's Department, on the
drafting of the first legislation submitted
to the Australian Parliament in 1901

BACKGROUND

It is an unfortunate fact of life that many leaders in business, in government and in the learned professions lack one very important skill - the ability to communicate effectively with their target audiences in a way which these can understand.

EXAMPLES

To illustrate, consider this extract from an actual letter from a leading firm of accountants to one of its clients:

> "Through focusing on the company's objectives, Critical Success Factors (CSFs) and risk profile we can determine an optimal audit/review approach and resource requirements and skills to ensure maximum value is realised from the function."

A helpful message from the Australian Taxation Office read as follows:

> "Superannuation contributions surcharge transfers - common reporting errors: There are a number of common errors that arise when reporting transfers. These errors cause reverse workflows. Listed is the common errors that are occurring and an explanation of how to correctly report transfers."

Even legislation is not free from incomprehensible jargon - for example:

> "A car is a predecessor of a second car if a third car is a predecessor of the second car and the first-mentioned car is a predecessor of the third car (including a case where the first-mentioned car is a predecessor of the third car by another application or applications of this paragraph)." - Income Tax Assessment Act 1936, section 82KTJ(4)(b).

The non-profit sector is just as bad. A recent media release for a festival read as follows:

> "A dance Improvisation exploring Labans Energy concept of Space; utilizing direct or indirect focus within the self, room and beyond."

Of course, even dictionaries sometimes let their readers down. Thus Webster's Seventh New Collegiate Dictionary defines "gyroscope" in the following terms:

> "A wheel or disk mounted to spin rapidly about an axis and also free to rotate about one or both of two axes perpendicular to each other and the axis of spin so that a rotation of one of the two mutually perpendicular axes results from application of torque to the other when the wheel is spinning and so that the entire apparatus offers considerable opposition depending on the angular momentum to any torque that would change the direction of the axis of spin."

The investment world has its problems, too. A recent review of investment managers contained the sentence: "Optimisation is used to maximise outperformance under forecast return scenarios."

Of course, these problems are not confined to Australia. The United Kingdom Home Office's guidance notes for the Crime and Disorder Bill 1998 included this brilliant passage:

> "Non Co Terminus Agency Boundaries: It will be up to each partnership to agree internally how it can best tackle the difficulties which would be thrown up by a lack of co terminusity. The goal should be for every partner to configure its output in such a way as to maximise effectiveness without promising the individual agencies wider strategic goals."

It is probably too much to expect literacy in Internet newsgroups. A recent posting read as follows:

> "... the very idea of participating in such revolutionary technological (to use a very limited term) transition is so exciting that I find myself speculating in many rather contradictory directions, leading along inconsistent paths ..."

A few further examples are worth quoting in this context:

> "... the cost savings achieved through close cluttering due to the nature of the products; for example, whether they are specialised products with a high information content, the nature of agglomeration economies and whether existing or potential externalities exist through common use of indivisible factor outputs ..." - Report of a Task Force on Employment and Unemployment
>
> "A theory which sees language as social activity and describes it in terms of systems of meaningful options." - Macquarie Dictionary, trying to define "systemic linguistics"

"The existing Environmental Management Policy is considered an appropriate umbrella vehicle to encapsulate the gambit of environmental matters including energy rather than formalise a separate energy policy." - the acting head of a large Australian research organisation

"This paradigm shift in the company's underlying fundamentals going forward is a direct outcome of inter-departmental cross fertilisation within the strict cost parameters set down for our growth driven diversification that is tracking to expectations and projecting value forward for our shareholders." - from the annual report of a company listed on the Australian Stock Exchange

"In our opinion, where the shareholders do not approve the resolutions, the advantages of approving the proposal will substitute as the disadvantages of not approving the proposal. Similarly, if the shareholders do not approve the proposal, it is our view that the disadvantages associated with the approval will substitute for the advantages of not approving the proposal." - from the explanatory memorandum accompanying a listed company's notice of meeting

"We are also talking real partnerships: Shell and others in the private sector innovating affordable locally relevant solutions; local customer and civil society groups being deeply involved in local energy distribution approaches that ensure both access for the poor and conservation; and governments, often with limited administrative capacity, that nevertheless create a policy environment that both keep energy affordable for the poor consumer while ensuring the energy producer the return necessary to stay in business." - from a Shell annual report to shareholders

"Six Sigma is a rigorous and a systematic methodology that utilises information (management by facts) and statistical analysis to measure and improve a company's operational performance, practices and systems by identifying and preventing 'defects' in manufacturing and service-related processes in order to anticipate and exceed expectations of all stakeholders to accomplish effectiveness." - from the ISixSigma company's web site

"Reduce jargon in all knowledge initiative documentation and presentation." - from a consultant's report to a government department, quoted by Don Watson

"Creativity expresses ideas in word, pigment or pixels and education, habits of reflection and powers of analysis allow exchanges of ideas without strife. Intellectual combat, of a constructive kind, is necessary to all the subtle accommodations in life being doctrinaire." - Justice Susan Crennan of the High Court of Australia

"A reference in a clause of this determination to particular information about the fund relating to a period prior to the publication date of the KFS includes a reference to the same information about a predecessor fund relating to the same period if the trustee believes, on reasonable grounds, that the characteristics of the predecessor fund are materially similar to the characteristics of the fund to such a degree that it is fair and accurate to treat the predecessor fund as the fund for the purposes of the clause ..." - A Determination by the former Insurance and Superannuation Commission

"As the cases of the degeneracy of France under the Fronde-allied Louis XIV, and the Fronde-like mentality of the profeudalist Physiocrats, of the ultra-reactionary Holy Alliance, there has been a persisting struggle throughout globally extended modern European civilization, between the defenders of the general welfare and those reactionaries who seek to return the planet as a whole to a more or less globalized sort of neo-feudalism, in which the majority of the those populations permitted to survive, are subjected to grab-your-forelocks-when-the-master-passes status as virtual human cattle." - Lyndon H LaRouche Jr

INTERESTING QUOTATIONS

All the above quotations were genuine attempts to communicate. However, some tongue-in-cheek examples also deserve a mention:

> "What we call 'language' is, in fact, a formal collective of imprecise verbal signals that serve as oblique coefficients of intuitive states wedded to analytical and discursive figurations of thought, and secondarily referential to perceived experience." - Sandra Boynton in *Don't let the Turkeys get you down*
>
> "In such a pragmatic, pluralist society, traditions and ways of life requiring for their successful reproduction more than protection of the rule of law and the provision of opportunity for meaningful participation in public life for those with few resources are allowed to wither." - from a forthcoming book
>
> "Don't overutilise ostentatiously pretentious language to delineate the thematic observations you are endeavoring to articulate." - the Fiske Guide to Getting into the Right College

And, in conclusion, a fine example of repeating oneself twice - a Channel 7 television programme entitled: "Prophecy Prediction - Into the Future"

CHAPTER 5

Gender Neutral Language

The only thing I was fit for was to be a writer,
and this notion rested solely on my suspicion
that I would never be fit for real work, and
that writing didn't require any

- Russell Baker

BACKGROUND

This chapter has drawn on material in the author's book Guide for Meetings and Organisations: Volume 1: Voluntary Associations, *published by the Law Book Company.*

THE PROBLEM

The absence of single words for the phrases "he or she", "his or her" and the like has long been a feature of the English language. In practice the masculine words are normally used, on the understanding that in many contexts these words embrace the feminine also.

Thus, for example, this book deliberately contains the briefer form "his" in numerous comments such as "It is highly desirable that the real author of a letter should sign it in his own name rather than in the name of some superior." To use "his or her" in such sentences, while clearly technically correct, could easily distract from the main point being made.

Sexist language can be encountered in most walks of life. Thus for instance a typical news item might read:

> "Each person present was invited to give his views on ..."

Again, a clause in an insurance policy might state:

> "A policyholder not paying his premium by the due date shall ..."

There are also frequently used expressions such as "the chairman of the meeting" and numerous words such as "statesman".

In fact, legal documents frequently have specific interpretation or definition clauses on the following lines:

> "In this Deed, unless the contrary intention appears, each gender includes each other gender ..."

just as they often go on to say:

> "and the singular number includes the plural and vice versa."

Even where such provisions are not explicitly included they would be implied.

Notwithstanding this, some people object to the use of so-called "sexist" language on the grounds that it suggests that only males are expected to be involved and that such terms thus reinforce male stereotypes and subliminally encourage discrimination against females. Such persons urge the use of what might be called "gender neutral" language.

THE SOLUTION

In these circumstances, it seems best not to invite the objections and to adopt instead a drafting style which avoids the problem. This can be done in a variety of ways, for example, by using the plural, as in "All electors shall cast their votes ..." rather than "Each elector shall cast his vote ...".

Care should, however, be taken to be grammatical and to avoid mixing singular and plural terms, as in "Each elector shall cast their vote ..." or, worse still, as in "Every candidate shall supply a photograph of themself ..."! Care should also be taken to avoid ambiguities.

However, the plural would not always make sense. For example, a Standing Order governing the conduct of a meeting and dealing with "a mover and his motion" from its nature needs to be cast in the singular. Phrases such as "a mover and the mover's motion" or "a mover and his or her motion", although clumsy, might need to be used in such circumstances.

Frequent repetition of such phrases can sound ungainly; no doubt this led long ago to the practice of using "he" when "he or she" was meant.

On a different aspect, the idiomatic form for the above-mentioned phrase is "his or her", putting the masculine term first, rather than the alphabetical "her or his" favoured by some theorists. This also applies to the common phrase in circular letters "Dear Sir or Madam".

It should be noted, however, that - in contrast to this - the feminine term is used first in the long-standing expression, "Ladies and Gentlemen". The form "his or her" is also used in some modern legislation.

The word "Chairman" is often used as the description of the head of a company or a public body. The word has for a very long time also been used as the customary title of the person presiding over a meeting. As with so much else in the lore of meetings procedure, this usage is steeped in tradition. Despite appearances, the word can be used for incumbents of either sex. As a form of address the title becomes either "Mr Chairman" or "Madam Chairman" (as the case may be).

Similarly, the even more masculine-sounding term "Lord Mayor" can be used for either sex.

The words "Chairwoman" for a female presiding officer and "Chairperson" for a presiding officer of either sex are neologisms of no philological merit whatsoever. The simultaneous use of "Chairman" for a male incumbent and "Chairperson" for a female incumbent is even sillier. Should an audience really be addressed as "Persons and Gentlemen"?

Like remarks apply to other similarly coined words - for example, "spokesperson" for "spokesman". (Surely those who think that the word "chairman" sounds unduly sexist should be equally offended by the "son" ending of "chairperson"?)

One solution to this dilemma is to use the term "Chair" (spelt with a capital letter) for the presiding officer. The word "chair", without the capital, can then be used for the symbol of authority rather than for the particular incumbent for the time being, as in phrases such as "asking all questions through the chair". However, there is some overlap between these two concepts. But this approach also has some limitations - the art of "chairmanship" cannot be termed "chairship".

Of course, in many contexts it is possible to use gender neutral expressions without the style sounding too artificial. Material can usually be drafted in non-sexist terms. For example:

- "mail officer" can be used instead of "mailman"
- "principal" can be used instead of "headmaster"
- "member of the committee" or "office-bearer" can be used rather than "committeeman"
- "president" (in relation to organisations) or "presiding officer" (in relation to meetings) can be used instead of "chairman".

However, terms such as "he/she" or artificial words such as "(s)he" should never be used.

If the plural is inappropriate then it may be feasible to cast a sentence in the passive voice or to use a simple "the" or "a" rather than either "his" or the fuller "his or her", as in "each person voting shall raise a hand" instead of "each person voting shall raise his hand".

Tedium can be reduced by varying the style - for example, by repeating the noun sometimes, by using "he or she" sometimes, and so on (although this may spoil the homogeneity of a list). For example:

"The secretary shall first present the secretary's report to the conference and the treasurer shall then give his or her analysis of the accounts."

However, once again internal consistency is most essential. An acceptable style can involve the use either of "he" or of "he or she", but not of a mixture.

FEMININE DESIGNATIONS

Nouns denoting persons fall into three categories:

- Those with separate forms for male and female - for example, *actor, actress; executor, executrix.* This group includes many words derived from other languages where different suffixes according to gender are normal, as well as English words ending in "-man" or "-master", "-woman" or "-mistress".
- Those with a common form for both - for example, *doctor, solicitor.*
- Those for which separate forms exist but for which the female version is generally not favoured - for example, *author, authoress; typist, typiste.* It is preferable that the male version should be used for either sex in such cases.

The expression "maiden name", which is used on many forms, seems inoffensive. In theory it could be replaced by some other phrase - for example, "birth name" - but the use of such an unfamiliar label might lead to confusion.

Any enthusiasm to find gender-neutral synonyms should have regard to linguistic considerations. For example, to remove the female-sounding suffix in "midwife" would be a nonsense. The word is cognate with the German *mit Weib*, meaning "with woman", in reference to the sex of the mother giving birth, not the sex of the person in attendance on her.

HOMOSEXUALITY

The term "homosexual" refers to both sexes; it is not the masculine of "lesbian". The root is the Greek *homos*, meaning "the same", not the Latin *homo*, meaning "man".

It is interesting to note that sometimes existing words are given new meanings for political reasons. Consider, for example, the long-established adjective *gay*. This was deliberately adopted as a synonym for "homosexual", in the hope that its employment would reduce prejudice. The strategy succeeded so well that many people no longer dare use the word in its traditional sense.

MAN

The desire for political correctness needs to be tempered in the case of well-established and especially poetic expressions. Thus to render "the brotherhood of man" as "the siblinghood of persons" would be absurd.

QUOTATIONS

John Donne wrote the famous and oft-quoted passage:

> "No man is an island, entire of itself... any man's death diminishes me, because I am involved in mankind; and therefore never send to know for whom the bell tolls; it tolls for thee."

Somehow, a rewritten version would not sound nearly as good: "No man or woman is an island, entire of itself..."

Furthermore, to mangle a classical quotation in such a way would interfere with the moral rights of its author.

SEX AND GENDER

The word "gender" is a grammatical term. It refers to masculine, feminine and neuter nouns, pronouns and adjectives - for example, *testator, testatrix*; *he, she* and *it.*

It should not be used as a synonym or a euphemism for "sex" when discussing male or female persons or animals.

CHAPTER 6

Badly Worded Resolutions

Oscar Wilde claimed the ability to make an instant pun about any subject. Someone challenged him with the word "queen". Wilde responded with: "The Queen is not a subject."

BACKGROUND

Thousands of formal meetings are held in Australia each year, involving the members of organisations ranging from small social groups to large public companies listed on the stock exchange, from trade unions to branches of political parties and from two dollar family companies to municipal corporations with multi-million dollar annual budgets.

All these meetings make decisions by passing resolutions. For practical and legal reasons all such resolutions need to be expressed in words. However, very little has been written about the techniques that should be employed when drafting proposals for consideration at such formal meetings.

As the various examples which follow show it is all too easy to compose a badly worded motion. These examples are all based on real life experiences. Naturally, the principles used in the redrafts shown here have general application.

RESOLUTIONS

1. "That this meeting set up a committee to investigate gambling and to function as follows:

   (a) The Executive shall draw up precise terms of reference.

   (b) The President shall appoint a convenor and two other members.

   (c) The Committee shall report to the next meeting.

   (d) Invite members to give evidence.

   (e) Instruct the Secretary to advise members accordingly.

   (f) And the meeting further authorises the Committee to liaise with any similar committees set up by other branches."

This should read:

> "That this meeting:
>
> (a) set up a committee to investigate gambling, the Committee to function as follows:
>
> (i) The Executive shall draw up precise terms of reference.
>
> (ii) The President shall appoint a convenor and two other members.
>
> (iii) The Committee shall report to the next meeting.
>
> (b) invite members to give evidence;
>
> (c) instruct the Secretary to advise members accordingly;
>
> (d) authorise the Committee to co-operate with any similar committees set up by other branches."

2. "The trade unions cannot be dissociated from politics and that it is unreal to attempt to do so."

This motion should probably read:

> "That, as part of the function of trade unions is to obtain legislative action as a result of political representation, this meeting urge the Government to refrain from any action making this more difficult."

But perhaps the motion means something else.

3. "This meeting affirms its appreciation of Mr Smith's action in continuing as Librarian. This action - which it feels certain will be appreciated by all members - will considerably assist the committee. This meeting is aware that books have been stolen in recent weeks for which it is not responsible. It believes, however, that this could be partly attributable to the caretaker's negligence."

This motion, which consists of four sentences, contains explanatory material which is best eliminated. It also contains a libel.

It could be reworded thus:

> "That this meeting:
>
> (a) affirm its appreciation of Mr Smith's action in continuing as Librarian;
>
> (b) record its regret that, due to circumstances beyond its control, books have been stolen in recent weeks;
>
> (c) urge the replacement of the current caretaker."

4. "That telephone subscribers may, if they so desire, and by right, be enabled to pay accounts by monthly instalments. No additional charge to be made for this. Provided that no instalment is less than $50."

This would read better as:

> "That telephone subscribers be permitted to pay accounts by monthly instalments without additional charge, provided that no instalment be less than $50."

5. "That to meet the need for higher productivity it is the considered opinion that the solution would lie in the adoption of a lower tax scale."

This would read better as:

> "That, to meet the need for higher productivity, taxes be lowered."

6. "That it be a punishable offence to leave small children alone in houses where there has been disastrous results."

This probably means:

> "That, in view of certain recent accidents, it be made a punishable offence to leave small children alone in houses."

7. "That we view with great concern the increase in accidents involving stationary trucks. We advise having more parking bays made. If trucks must stop in other places to have suitable sign 25 metres to rear of vehicle."

This could be reworded to:

> "That this meeting:
>
> (a) record its great concern at the increase in accidents involving stationary trucks;
>
> (b) recommend the construction of more parking bays;
>
> (c) urge legislation compelling any truck forced to stop in other places to erect a suitable sign 25 metres behind the vehicle."

8. "That the trams are always overcrowded."

This motion may have been designed merely to place on record an existing state of affairs, but more probably its movers sought some improvement. A more constructive motion would have been:

> "That the Government take steps to eliminate the present excessive overcrowding of trams by legislating for staggered hours and by granting financial assistance to the Tramways Board to enable it to get more rolling stock and staff."

9. "That the price of eggs should not increase; and the Government to watch this problem."

This should read:

"That the Egg Board be urged not to increase the price of eggs and the Government be asked to watch this problem."

10. "That section 12 of the *Broadcasting Act* be repealed."

This motion is meaningless unless the reader has the Act. A more helpful motion would be:

"That the section of the *Broadcasting Act* which restricts the setting-up of more country stations be repealed."

A motion referring to section 12 of the organisation's new Constitution would, however, be in order. Members can be deemed to have ready access to the document involved. Furthermore, an amendment to the body's Constitution can be made only in this necessarily formal way.

11. "That the price of beer is high."

This could mean one of several things:

(a) If "is" is merely a mistake for "be", it could mean:

"That the price of beer be made high."

(b) If "high" has been used as short for "too high", it could mean the opposite:

"That the price of beer be reduced."

(c) If the motion is meant to be neutral, it could mean:

"That the fact that the price of beer is high be recorded in the minutes."

12. "That earnest consideration should once again be given to the establishment of an Upper House. This should be comprised of half men (not unsuccessful politicians) and half women."

It is not clear what definition of "unsuccessful politicians" the mover has in mind. A suggested rewording of the motion is as follows:

"That earnest consideration should once again be given to the establishment of an Upper House, on the basis of equal representation of both sexes, and with a suitable entrance qualification to ensure that no member is chosen merely through suffering defeat in a Lower House poll."

13. "That a letter be written to Mr Smith re payment for house painting."

This patently ambiguous motion should be appropriately reworded - for example to:

"... demanding payment of $100 within 7 days in respect of the painting of his house" or

"... waiving the payment for painting his house".

14. "That the Government give this Club $1,000."

This naive motion, even if passed by a club, is likely to be abortive and is thus pointless. It should be replaced by a more positive motion: for example, one authorising an appropriate detailed submission to a relevant Minister and calling for some alternative action in the event of an unfavourable response.

15. "That the committee set up a Club Library, to be a reasonable size."

This motion raises many more questions than it answers:

- What does "reasonable" mean, in terms of either a number of books or a total cost?
- Is the size meant to be "reasonable" in relation to the surplus cash held, in relation to the size of the membership, or in relation to the expected usage?
- Is the library meant to be a reference library or one that lends books either to members only or to both members and outsiders?
- Or is it to act as a quasi-museum for archival or historical material?
- How are the books to be housed?

- Should the library stock be built up quickly, or gradually over, say, the next ten years?
- Should the stock include non-book material?
- How is the library to be staffed?
- Who is to do the cataloguing?

16. "That the Nominating Committee be the sole arbiter of fair and legitimate conduct during an election campaign."

This motion is unsatisfactory in that it does not define "fair and legitimate conduct" or give any yardstick by which such conduct could be judged. (Presumably the motion does not refer to irregularities in the conduct of the election itself, which would normally be the responsibility of the Returning Officer.)

The motion is also unsatisfactory because it does not spell out the remedies to apply in the case of unacceptable conduct:

- Should the candidates concerned be disqualified?
- If so, by whom and subject to what safeguards and appeal machinery?
- Should they be ordered to desist from their conduct, under threat of disqualification if they do not?
- Should the organisation provide some form of redress to the remaining candidates?
- Should the election be either postponed or abandoned?
- Or should the Nominating Committee merely use moral suasion?
- Should the position be different if *all* candidates are equally guilty?

A motion on the above lines would need to be ruled out of order as being far too vague for such an important subject.

17. "Each candidate at the time of lodging their nomination shall supply the Returning Officer with a recent photograph of themself."

The grammar leaves something to be desired. The singular word "each" should not be followed by the plural form "their" and, of course, there is no such word as "themself". This motion could be reworded to read:

> "That each candidate at the time of lodging his or her nomination be required to provide the Returning Officer with a recent passport-style photograph of the candidate."

18. "That, say, $1,000 be spent on this campaign."

The word "say" makes the motion useless as authority for the spending of money. A motion using "up to $..." would achieve the desired purpose.

19. "There may be occasions where there is a minor deviation from official policy. It is not the membership's intention that policy should be slavishly followed under all circumstances. Therefore it was *resolved* that reasonable discretion can be exercised. However, common sense must prevail in approving any deviation. Whoever departs from policy should be satisfied that the attractions of so doing are sufficient to warrant the deviation and that if approval was to be sought from a meeting it would be reasonably certain of approval."

The deficiencies in this minute are so gross and so obvious that detailed comment seems superfluous.

20. "That this annual general meeting of the Smithville Protest Group held in the Smithville Town Hall.

    "Gives notice of their opposition to and calls for a fully informed public debate on the recent Jones Committee Recommendations.

    "We accept the fact that there is room for some structuring of the Transport Industry we should therefore be looking for an alternative to privatisation."

This is another inelegant motion, which could be rewritten on the following lines:

> "That this annual general meeting of the Smithville Protest Group held in the Smithville Town Hall:
>
> (a) record its opposition to the recent report of the Jones Committee;
>
> (b) call for a fully-informed public debate on its recommendations;
>
> (c) accept the fact that there is room for some restructuring of the transport industry;
>
> (d) urge the government to seek an alternative to privatisation."

AMENDMENTS TO RESOLUTIONS

Problems can also arise when persons move amendments to motions before the chair, especially if the desired changes have not been thought through beforehand.

Consider, for example, a meeting which has before it a routine resolution such as "That the accounts be adopted."

An amendment as follows might be proposed from the floor:

> "That the following words be added at the end of the resolution:
>
> 'but that, having regard to the fact that the company's earning rate on its shareholders' funds was only 3 per cent last year, the board be requested to institute as a matter of urgency a suitable program of asset disposals in order to lift the earning rate to at least the level being attained by the company's major competitors.'"

Said quickly, this probably sounds reasonable enough. However, such an amendment would actually leave the existing full stop before the new words, which would be an unintended nonsense.

A better form of words for the amendment would be:

"That the full stop at the end of the resolution be omitted and that the following be inserted in its place:

', but that, having regard to the fact that the company's earning rate on its shareholders' funds was only 3 per cent last year, the board be requested to institute as a matter of urgency a suitable program of asset disposals in order to lift the earning rate to at least the level being attained by the company's major competitors.'"

CHAPTER 7

Some Management Issues

By being in the lowest form I gained an immense advantage over the cleverer boys. They all went on to learn Latin and Greek, but I was taught English.

- Winston Churchill

SLOPPY BUSINESS PRACTICES

While the opening chapters of this book were primarily concerned to raise standards in regard to the written work of individuals a few comments on some related management issues might be worth mentioning.

For instance, some organisations fail to recruit staff wisely or to train and supervise their employees adequately.

Some habitually do not reply to letters or e-mails. Others take an inordinately long time to respond, but do not bother to pay their correspondents the elementary courtesy of sending either an acknowledgement or an interim reply.

Many businesses seem to have a policy of not returning telephone calls, a problem possibly made worse by the habit of some operators, when noting a caller's details, not to take the simple precaution of reading these back to ensure their accuracy.

Customers might well assume that, if an organisation is inefficient in regard to telephone calls, then it is probably inefficient all round.

The cost of fixing up errors after they are made - or of not fixing them up at all and living with the consequences - is often many times greater than if proper steps to prevent the errors had been taken in the first place. Apart from direct financial consequences, mistakes often result in a loss of customer goodwill and in a sceptical response to subsequent advice from the organisation concerned even when such information happens to be accurate.

The lower productivity resulting from poor management practices also hurts the nation as a whole.

CREDIBILITY

The printed page and web pages on the Internet both carry a surprising degree of authority, which may or may not be justified in any particular case. However, this is only the prima facie position. Readers will always judge material by having regard to what they already know.

If they see eight statements and know at first hand that three are factual then they will readily believe the other five. If, on the other hand, they see eight statements and know at first hand that three are wrong then they will probably not even bother to read the rest of the material, let alone believe it or act on it.

Again, if some written piece is full of glaring typographical errors then its producers will have an unnecessary problem on their hands. Its readers will think that if the typing or printing have not been checked properly then the facts have probably not been checked out either.

Some attempts to gain credibility are almost laughable. To illustrate:

If the promoters of a "get rich quick" scheme say that its legality has been "confirmed by the media", what does that actually mean? Who, in what publication, really said what? And what were the unnamed writer's qualifications?

Again, if a catalogue from a store says, in relation to some product, "as seen on TV", does that mean any more than that "we paid to advertise this on television"? This phony invocation of authority says nothing about the quality of the goods or the value for money which they represent.

THE ROLE OF EMPLOYERS

Apparently, many employers no longer care whether their own staffs can write passable English. They probably think that it does not really matter.

Perhaps they share the current view of many educators that to teach formal grammar is an outdated concept of little pedagogical value or relevance.

Actually, employees who are only semi-literate can cost their employers a lot of money - as, for example, when staff fail to produce:

- meaningful correspondence
- effective sales material
- understandable manuals, or even
- valid contracts.

If junior employees lack the necessary skills then that will create even bigger problems as they advance to positions of greater responsibility in later life.

Writing in a typical company situation needs to address a range of different target audiences - present and potential customers, fellow workers, official bodies, and so on. The style always needs to match the actual circumstances.

An organisation's image is also important in marketing situations. It is not enhanced if typographical or stylistic errors are left uncorrected or if ignorance of the fundamental rules governing the English language is displayed.

While individual employers obviously lack the capacity to rectify basic defects in the Australian education system, they can still help themselves in various ways. For instance, they can:

- organise specially designed "plain English" courses for their staffs
- institute semi-formal on-the-job training
- produce their own in-house style manuals
- evolve approved standard wordings for key letters
- provide their employees with ready access to a wide range of appropriate reference books.

A serious problem is now facing the community. Executives who are only semi-literate themselves are often unaware of that fact. They probably recruit junior employees using criteria other than their skills with the English language. These in turn, as they pass through the ranks, will make further appointments of people like themselves.

SOME CASE STUDIES

In the same way as a picture is worth a thousand words a few case studies are presented below in order to illustrate some of the principles discussed above.

CASE 1: BLAMING THE COMPUTER

Many business letters involve a lack of logic, extreme arrogance, a patronising air and/or just plain stupidity and incompetence on the part of their authors.

For example, a well-known lending institution wrote to one of its home purchase borrowers in the following terms (liberally sprinkling its text with stray commas in the process):

> From this month, we have changed to a new E.D.P. System, which unfortunately can not cope effectively with quarterly instalments, on "Interest Only" loans. "The System", drew on your Account, in November for your quarterly amount of $958.50 and the program is such, that we can not prevent monthly drawings.

When replying, the recipient - who did not suffer fools gladly - was forced to comment:

> Quite apart from its appalling punctuation and grammar, your letter's reference to "The System" in capitals and inverted commas as though it were some deity is really quite astonishing. Surely "The System" to the customer is just "the company".
>
> This system must have been drawn up by human beings paid for by the company and to its instructions. It is not something extraneous that can be expected to behave in an unpredictable way.
>
> I cannot understand how in this day and age you can set up a new computer system which is so poorly designed that it cannot even deal with perfectly standard contracts which are already on your books. Would it not be preferable to fix up the program rather than ask customers to vary the agreed arrangements and in the process incur higher costs? Should not, in any case, the program be made more flexible in order to be able to cope with future developments?

The common practice of blaming the computer for every human error and for any inability to meet legitimate customer requests for service or information is, of course, quite unacceptable.

CASE 2: SNOWING THE CUSTOMER

In a different category again are unsophisticated marketing communications. A gross example follows. A recent circular issued by an insurance company in order to induce its readers to buy more life insurance started off its sales spiel with a completely irrelevant story:

> ... in 1931 Dame Nellie Melba, the world's leading soprano of her time, died in Sydney, her last words being two bars from "Ave Maria". On that same day in 1970 the Indian Pacific made its inaugural transcontinental journey.

Actually, the main message of this circular was to the effect that it was cheaper to buy life insurance *before* rather than *after* a birthday (in this case, the anniversary of the events described above).

This is fair enough - but the circular did not go on to say:

- why its recipient should buy any life insurance at all
- why, even if the recipient did, the policy should be "whole of life" - a label which, incidentally, the circular carefully avoided
- why that particular company's products, which allowed it to increase future premiums, should be chosen over those of its competitors which involved guaranteed rates
- why the ideal sum insured was the $8,000 being offered - there was no trace of the "know your client" formula favoured in modern financial circles!

CASE 3: SHEER ARROGANCE

A commercial organisation was caught out in imposing a series of illegal charges on a customer. Instead of conceding graciously and apologising, it just wrote to the customer to the effect that his account had been credited and that similar charges in the future "will also be waived".

It did not seem to have occurred to that organisation that something to which it was never entitled cannot actually be "waived".

The customer was then asked to confirm in writing that he was satisfied with this "offer"!

CASE 4: A FORM FOR THE ELDERLY

The application form for the Seniors Card – a useful State Government initiative for Victorian residents aged 60 years or over – contained the following confusing question which puzzled many elderly people:

> I am not in the full-time workforce Yes ... No ...

Should the correct answer for a retired person have been:

- "Yes, I am not in the full-time workforce" or
- "No, I am not in the full-time workforce"?

WHAT DOES A "GUARANTEED" INVESTMENT REALLY MEAN?

Most investors know that when they get investment advice from a stockbroker or a financial planner it is based on value judgements and that the advice thus comes without guarantees of any sort.

However, the word "guaranteed" is thrown about in many investment contexts and frequently involves misunderstandings. For example, many people mistakenly believe that bank deposits are somehow guaranteed by the Federal government or its central bank.

Such deposits are not so guaranteed at all. They are really just unsecured loans to a private company, an entity which while large could fail in the same way as any other private company could, through fraud or mismanagement, and, indeed, as a British bank (Barings) did not so long ago. In recent times many Asian banks have been in deep trouble.

All that the Reserve Bank of Australia in this country does is to supervise the banking system as a whole and to express a willingness to help out an individual bank if it is solvent but ever has a temporary liquidity crisis.

Then there are the investment bonds which are widely being marketed as "capital guaranteed". Usually this just means that they are backed by fixed interest securities the capital value of which is unlikely to fluctuate much.

Investment advertisements should always be read critically. Whenever anything is said to be "guaranteed" several important questions arise:

- Precisely what is being guaranteed? For example, is it capital or income or both? Does the guarantee apply at all times or can it be called upon only once on some defined future day, possibly many years away?
- Just how strong is the guarantor in relation to the sums actually being guaranteed? If a $5,000 company "guarantees" the repayment of a $250 million debt then that guarantee is hardly worth having. A guarantee is only as good as its guarantor.

On a slightly different aspect, it is also nonsensical for the contractual obligations of some entity to be "guaranteed" by the entity itself - the word implies a promise by a third party.

Subsidiaries and associates of listed companies are sometimes listed companies in their own right and/or engage in borrowing from the general public. The name of the subsidiary or associate company may or may not resemble that of the parent company. It may or may not be using the parent company's logo.

It should be noted that in the absence of specific guarantees or other contractual arrangements there is no legal obligation on a parent company to assist persons who may be investors in, or creditors of, one of its subsidiaries if such an entity ever gets into financial trouble. In fact, the primary obligation on company directors is to look after the interests *of their own shareholders.*

However, depending on the circumstances, a parent company may, of course, regard itself as having a *moral* duty to bail out persons who dealt with a subsidiary in the belief that the parent company would always stand behind it.

Prospectuses and publicity material for futures funds and other highly speculative ventures sometimes feature a guarantee of some sort in order to make the scheme concerned sound more attractive to conservative investors.

Special attention is drawn to one aspect of this theme - a guarantee from, say, a bank or some other highly reputable institution to the effect that the investors will get all of the original invested amount back at the end of a certain period, say seven years.

This is made possible by placing about half of each investor's stake in safe fixed interest paper (possibly a zero coupon stock) and using only the balance for the speculative purposes featured by the promoter.

At about 10 per cent per annum compound interest, money doubles in seven years, so nothing particularly outstanding is involved in any such arrangements. It is important to note that such guarantees usually operate only at the end of the stipulated term. They thus do little to protect investors wishing to quit before then.

A guarantee on these lines is sound enough - but hardly free of cost. Merely getting one's own money back without return and without adjustment for inflation is no great bargain.

In any case, any investors so minded can replicate such an arrangement themselves. If they are prepared to forego all annual return for some years then they can ensure the preservation of their capital in dollar terms by putting half of the funds into some safe interest-bearing security and reinvesting the interest, exposing only the other half to any investment risk.

While such arrangements may have a certain amount of marketing appeal, there is a distinct lack of logic behind them. Why should an investor who is looking for the excitement and potential gains of some speculative venture and who desires to back the entrepreneurial judgement of the promoter concerned be forced to put about half of the stake into decidedly dull fixed interest securities?

Having to pay relatively high initial and ongoing fees for the privilege of investing in such paper only makes the whole proposition even less attractive. Promoters wishing to offer such a guarantee to their more timid customers would attract more business from others if the guarantee instead of being compulsory were merely an optional extra.

Again, some cash management trusts involve a guarantee from a related company in respect of the face value of the units and all previously declared interest. However, unless the shareholders' funds of that company are large in relation to the trust fund then that guarantee may not be particularly meaningful.

Government loans are usually marketed as "guaranteed". They can indeed be regarded as risk-free in the sense that the regular payment of interest on the due dates and the repayment of the capital on the stipulated maturity date are assured. However, three separate risks should be mentioned for the record.

- Firstly, if the Australian Government were ever overthrown by revolution or invasion, then the securities mentioned above would all become as worthless as Czarist loans. But in those circumstances every other asset in Australia would, of course, also suffer a similar fate.
- Secondly, the only contractual promises refer to punctual payment on the due dates. There is no guarantee that the market value during the currency of the loan will not fall to less than the issue price or the cost price to any subsequent purchaser. Market prices can, in fact, move up or down every day. Furthermore, there is no certainty that there will always be a convenient market on which orderly trading will take place or that a particular issue will be liquid on the stock exchange.
- Thirdly, the only contractual promises refer to a payment in Australian dollars. There is no undertaking

CHAPTER 8

Miscellaneous

With words we govern men

- Benjamin Disraeli

UNITED STATES USAGES

Many common concepts give rise to entirely different words in different parts of the English-speaking world. The following examples will illustrate this point:

United Kingdom Word	United States Word
autumn	fall
biscuits	cookies
boot (in cars)	trunk
braces	suspenders
chemist	druggist
footpath	sidewalk
pharmacist	druggist
postcode	zip code
Red Indian	American Indian
queue	line
tram	streetcar
underground (railway)	subway
zed	zee

A much larger list on these lines is included in David Crystal's excellent *Cambridge Encyclopedia of the English Language* (1999).

But unfortunately he gives only the British English equivalents of American English words starting with A to G and the American English equivalents of British English words starting with H to Z. Too bad if one wants to look up an American English word starting with H to Z or a British English word starting with A to G!

POOR COMMUNICATIONS

When a major bank uses as its self-promoting slogan the question "Who can you bank on?" it is presumably hoping that its name will spring to mind. However, the reaction from an educated ear is much more likely to be irritation and disgust.

The bank has obviously not realised it, but it is sending a message into the subconscious of the advertisement's readers - a loud and clear signal which says: "We have no standards", with overtones of "We are an ignorant mob and we couldn't care less". Is this really what the bank wants?

UNACCEPTABLE EDITORIAL LAPSES

Most readers will overlook minor blemishes in certain publications, particularly those being produced by small voluntary organisations on a shoestring in the spare time of a volunteer who is one of their fellow members.

However, sometimes the editorial lapses even in these are so great that they should not really be tolerated. Some examples based on a single issue of an actual publication will illustrate the point:

- The name of the publication was misspelt in the heading of the column giving editorial information.

- The standard of proofreading and spell checking were so poor that even blatant errors and internal inconsistencies went undetected.
- The publication did not bear a date.
- The front page gave no clue as to the identity of the organisation actually issuing the publication.

Worst of all, an interesting item was featured on page 1. It finished in mid-sentence with a note reading: "continued on page 3". The rest of the story was nowhere to be found on page 3 or, for that matter, anywhere else.

The likely effect of such ineptitude on readers can perhaps be demonstrated by the following illustrative article:

> *WHO KILLED THE NAKED BLACK LESBIAN?*
>
> A few hours after the adjournment of our long committee meeting last Wednesday night our beloved president was woken up at about four o'clock in the morning by a loud banging on her front door.
>
> With considerable annoyance she opened it and found two burly policemen on the doorstep, waving what seemed to be a warrant at her. Instead of apologising for the disturbance they went straight to the point:
>
> "Were you the per- (continued on page 5)

FOUL LANGUAGE

The common use of dashes or asterisks in a childish and half-hearted attempt to disguise words which some people might regard as obscene is really quite stupid and merely serves to draw extra attention to them.

Writers with a good vocabulary do not need to use vulgar expressions for their own text, but if they are quoting other persons or fictional characters then they should do so openly.

But at least Australians do not face penalties such as those imposed in some foreign jurisdictions. For example, in October

2005 a Turkish court fined 20 people for using the letters Q and W on placards written in Kurdish at a Kurdish new year celebration, under a law that bans the use of characters not in the Turkish alphabet. The letters Q and W (and X) do not exist in the Turkish alphabet.

NAMES FOR FAMILY COMPANIES AND TRUSTS

The current legislation no longer requires Australian companies to have names consisting of words. This reform eliminated the need to find a distinctive name which was not already in use, thus greatly simplifying the registration process.

Instead a company can, if its promoters so choose, now be known simply as "Australian Company Number ... Pty Ltd" or something similar.

Neither is there any legal provision requiring a family trust to have a distinct name. A trust can instead be referred to as having been constituted by a deed of settlement made on such-and-such a date between such-and-such parties.

However, a concise and distinctive name is administratively convenient, especially if a family is involved with more than one family trust. A name such as "Smith Family Trust" or "John Smith Family Trust" is frequently used, but if a common surname is involved even that can cause confusion.

Other alternatives would include:

- An arbitrary name - for example, "Wallaby Family Trust" or just "Wallaby Trust".
- A made-up word, possibly derived from the first names or the initials of the parties involved.
- A surname spelt backwards.
- A name belonging to some admired historical figure.
- A name based on the street address of one of the parties.
- A name already being used by one of the parties on the Internet.

The same approaches can be used for naming family companies.

SPAM

The word *spam* (in reference to unsolicited commercial e-mail or UCE) intrigues many people.

Spam is a great nuisance to many Internet users. Filtering can help on an individual level, but enormous costs from this unwanted bulk traffic are being imposed on the system as a whole.

It is believed that the term *spam* was derived from a famous Monty Python sketch on British television, which contained the following much-liked passage:

> *Waitress: "Well, there's ... egg and Spam; egg, bacon and Spam; egg, bacon, sausage and Spam; Spam, bacon, sausage and Spam; Spam, egg, Spam, Spam, bacon and Spam ..."*

The episode concerned also featured a song rendered by a chorus of Vikings, with numerous references to "spam, spam, glorious spam".

This episode was recalled when spam first began arriving over the Internet.

However, "SPAM" (written in capitals) is actually a registered trademark of Hormel Foods Corporation of Austin, Minnesota, United States, a company dating back to 1891 and now listed on the New York Stock Exchange.

PREPOSITIONS AT THE END OF SENTENCES

Sir Winston Churchill is reputed to have said once:

> *This is the sort of English up with which I will not put.*

or, in another version of the incident:

This is the sort of bloody nonsense up with which I will not put.

It is not clear whether the person rebuked by Churchill was an editor, a public servant, a correspondent or even a member of an audience when the great man gave a speech. Did Churchill write a note, scribble on an official document or say the words aloud?

It seems more likely that the story is only apocryphal. In any case, the remark is based on a misconception.

It is often not desirable to separate a preposition from the word it governs, because apart from being inelegant this does not aid comprehension. Thus

What logic is this conclusion reached by?

would not be as clear as

By what logic is this conclusion reached?

However, some short sentences do not suffer from this problem. For example:

Just what is this all about?

sounds all right.

The problem arises in sentences such as

Who is it by?

This should really be rendered as

By whom is it?

using the accusative case for the object of the preposition. However, the speaker probably desired to make "who" the subject, and accordingly a question such as

Who originated it?

might be better still.

It should be pointed out that not all words which look like prepositions are indeed prepositions. Some are parts of compound verbs.

To illustrate:

In the sentence:

I looked at Mary.

the verb is “to look at”, not “to look”. In fact, the construction is really similar to

I saw Mary.

as becomes obvious when the corresponding passive voice expressions are considered:

Mary was looked at by me.

Mary was seen by me.

In contrast:

I went to Melbourne.

does not give rise to a passive

Melbourne was gone to by me.

Here “to” is a true preposition, not a part of a compound verb.

Similarly:

This is something which she looked into.

is quite in order. It is parallel to

This is something which she studied.

Here “into” is not a preposition governing “which”; it is again part of a compound verb.

Reverting to the Churchill scenario, “put up with”, although comprising several words, is actually a compound verb which corresponds to “tolerate”. A sentence such as

It was put up with by us for years.

while not ideal does not seem outrageous.

Churchill's model:

This is the sort of English which I will not put up with.

could equally well have been rendered as

This is the sort of English which I will not tolerate.

- thus removing any problem.

DDMMYY

As computer users will know, the United States practice is to express dates in the quite illogical month-day-year (MMDDYY) format. To show the month, which comes between the day and the year in order of magnitude, in this way is clearly absurd. Australia and the rest of the world use either day-month-year (DDMMYY or DDMMYYYY) or year-month-day (YYMMDD or YYYYMMDD).

The fact that the United States clings to a non-uniform and ambiguous date format is quite absurd and does nothing for the image of that country as a technologically advanced nation.

But how did this strange practice originate?

The Library of Congress supplied the following comments:

> "It is probably not possible to answer this question definitively, since it appears that the prevalence of the month/day/year format in the US is a matter of custom and preference rather than the product of a discrete, documented historical event.
>
> "We have looked extensively in our collections, looking through books cataloged under the subjects 'Chronology' and related subject headings; numerous published compilations of questions and answers about culture and mores (such as David Feldman's 'Imponderables' series

and Cecil Adams' 'The Straight Dope'); 'Historical Abstracts', an index of journal articles in world history; and print and online indexes to newspaper and magazine articles and government documents from the 19th and 20th centuries.

"We have also consulted Stumpers, a listserv of difficult-to-answer reference questions submitted by librarians across the US. We have been unable to find any record of an official 'adoption' of the month/day/year format in the US.

"It may be possible to arrive at a supposition about the origin of the custom through the study of primary sources, especially British and American correspondence from the late 18th and early 19th centuries.

"An examination of the correspondence of Sir Joseph Banks (1743-1820) and Matthew Flinders (1774-1814) indicates that the British used both month/day/year and day/month/year formats in their correspondence during this period. We have been able to detect no pattern as to when each format is used, save for personal preference.

"For example, Governor Arthur Phillip tends to use the month/day/year formula in his letters to Banks, while Captain James Cook inclines toward day/month/year; Governor William Bligh uses either formula at various times. The Banks and Flinders correspondence has been digitised by the State Library of New South Wales and can be viewed at http://www.sl.nsw.gov.au/banks/ and http://www.sl.nsw.gov.au/flinders/ respectively.

"This also appears to be true of American correspondence from roughly the same period. Our perusal of the papers of early American statesmen George Washington, Thomas Jefferson and James Madison indicates that they and their correspondents used both month/day/year and day/month/year, albeit with a preference for the former. (Washington and John Hancock employ both formats in their letters, while the American general Artemas Ward consistently used day/month/year.)

"The papers of Washington, Jefferson and Madison have been digitised and are available on the Library of Congress web site via American Memory, http://memory.loc.gov/

"A definitive statement on this subject would probably require an extensive, systematic survey of unindexed primary source materials such as those described above. Unfortunately, due to the volume of requests we receive, the Library of Congress does not have the staff resources to undertake such extensive research for any one query.

"The preliminary evidence cited above would lead us to postulate that during the early years of American independence, the British and the Americans used both day/month/year and month/day/year formats when putting dates in writing. This begs (sic) the question of how and why the former became prevalent in Great Britain and its overseas possessions, while Americans inclined toward the latter over the years. As nearly as we can determine, that question has yet to be addressed in any published source."

BC/AD/BCE/CE

It has been customary, when referring to historical events, to specify that a year or a century is either BC ("before Christ", meaning before a very approximate date of Christ's birth) or AD (*anno domini*, Latin for "in the year of the Lord").

This nomenclature is well established, despite being unpopular with many non-Christians. However, most people in countries such as Australia are not particularly conscious of the religious connotations in these abbreviations. On the other hand, some persons are concerned that these labels could give offence to the adherents of some non-Christian faiths.

They have therefore started to use CE (for "common era") and BCE (for "before the common era"). These new abbreviations may be more politically correct, but they also seem to involve change for the sake of change.

Some problems are:

- The use of one symbol (CE) which is two characters long and another (BCE) three characters long is rather untidy.
- The letter "C" can easily be mistaken for "Christian".
- The two new symbols are not as distinct from each other as AD and BC are from each other.
- The departure from the conventional BC/AD symbols is offensive to some fundamental Christians.
- Some dictionaries do not even include the phrase "common era".
- It seems undesirable to use two different sets of notation for the same concept concurrently.

The International Organization for Standardization has laid down a standard, ISO 8601, which prescribes a new way for setting out dates. This is YYYY-MM-DD (for example, 2004-07-31), with the greatest unit being to the left, as in the case of ordinary numbers. However, BCE and CE are not recognised by ISO 8601.

Furthermore, the new notation fails to correct the major flaw of the present BC/AD system, namely, the absence of a year zero. This could be overcome by using CE with negative numbers in the same way as temperatures can involve negative numbers for degrees – see column (4) on the following page:

Column (1) is the traditional system.

Column (2) is a more consistent approach.

Column (3) is the system favoured by historians, secularists and others.

Column (4) is a more logical approach.

(1)	(2)	(3)	(4)
AD 3	3 AD	3 CE	3 CE
AD 2	2 AD	2 CE	2 CE
AD 1	1 AD	1 CE	1 CE
1 BC	1 BC	1 BCE	0 CE
2 BC	2 BC	2 BCE	-1 CE
3 BC	3 BC	3 BCE	-2 CE

ONLINE DICTIONARIES

The last appendix to this book inter alia lists the web addresses of a number of online dictionaries.

Particular attention is drawn to OneLook

http://www.onelook.com

which provides definitions from over 1000 different dictionaries.

In a different category is WordWeb. This is an excellent dictionary tool, but it needs to be installed on the user's computer. It can be found at

http://wordweb.info/free/

However, at this stage the author's *Dictionary of Stock Exchange and Investment Terms* (Bas Publishing, 2004) is available only in hard copy. It is dedicated "to all investors who don't know the difference between a green shoe and a black box".

FIRST GENERATION

Q. Does the expression "first generation" refer to persons who migrated to a new country or to their offspring?

A. Take your pick. Different dictionaries give different definitions. Some even given two contradictory explanations - for example, the American Heritage Dictionary of the English Language, Fourth Edition, 2000, says:

1. Of or relating to a person who has left one country and settled in another.
2. Of or relating to a person or persons whose parents are immigrants.

There is also a further angle: What generation is a person with one parent a migrant and the other parent, say, the grandchild of a migrant?

ENSURING THE ACCURACY OF LINKS

Many publications include references to links to various web sites which contain information likely to be of interest or relevance to their readers. Often the data on these sites will be updated periodically - an important advantage over the contents of a printed work.

However, one problem is the ephemeral nature of the Internet. Some web addresses get changed over time, while in other cases the pages are simply removed. Some addresses are rather long, increasing the scope for typographical errors which render the link completely useless. Manual checking can be time-consuming and tedious.

One solution is for the author to put all the links into a single appendix. This appendix can then be uploaded to an appropriate web site.

Once there the validity of all links can very quickly be checked electronically by using http://www.siteowner.com/badlinks.cfm

Any annoying "404" errors (page not found) can then be investigated and rectified.

Naturally, a final check should be carried out at the last possible moment before the publication concerned goes to the printer.

STATE AID FOR MOTORISTS

To conclude this chapter, an illustration of how ridicule can sometimes be used to make a political point.

In the late 1960s the Australian community was debating the funding of education. The author sent the following letter to the editor of a leading newspaper:

> "The time has surely come for serious consideration to be given to providing State Aid for motorists.
>
> "This is a matter of simple justice. It is unreasonable that persons owning private cars should be required to meet the running costs of these as well as to pay taxes to support a public transport system.
>
> "Because so many motorists drive their own cars the Government is saved the necessity of providing numerous additional trams and trains. It is also relieved of the need to find additional crews to run them. All this helps to cut down the losses on the public transport system.
>
> "Furthermore, the authorities would be greatly embarrassed if all the people who now use private cars suddenly switched to public transport. The community also benefits from the experimentation possible in the case of private vehicles but lacking in a governmental network.
>
> "State Aid for motorists would give proper recognition of the right of each citizen to choose for himself which transport system (public or private) is best for his individual needs."

PART II

FOR LOVERS OF WORDS

CHAPTER 9

How Many Words Are There In The English Language?

Slovenly language corrodes the mind

-John Q Adams

BACKGROUND

Just how many words are there in the English language? And how many does any one person know? This is an article by Michael Quinion <http://www.worldwidewords.org>. It is reprinted by permission.

COUNTING THE WORDS

One of the more common questions that arrive for the Q&A section asks how many words there are in the English language. Almost as common are requests for the average size of a person's vocabulary.

These sound like easy questions; I have to tell you that they're indeed easy to ask. But they're almost impossible to answer satisfactorily, because it all depends on what one means by *word* and by *vocabulary* (or even by *English*).

What we mean by *word* sounds obvious, but it's not. Take a verb such as *climb*. The rules of English allow you to generate the forms *climbs*, *climbed*, *climbable* and *climbing*, the nouns *climb* and *climber* (and their plurals *climbs* and *climbers*), compounds such as *climb-down* and *climbing frame*, and phrasal verbs such as *climb on*, *climb over* and *climb down*. Now, here's the question you have to answer: are all these distinct words, or do you lump them all together under *climb*?

That this is not a trivial question can be proved by looking at half a dozen current dictionaries. You won't find two that agree on what to list. Almost every word in the language has this fuzzy penumbra of inflected forms, separate senses and compounds, some to a much greater extent than *climb*. To take a famous case, the entry for *set* in the *Oxford English Dictionary* runs to 60,000 words. The noun alone has 47 separate senses listed. Are all these distinct words?

And, in a wider sense, what do you include in your list of words? Do you count all the regional variations of English? Or slang? Dialect? Family or private language? Proper names and the names of places? And what about abbreviations? The biggest dictionary of them has more than 400,000 entries - do you count them all as words? And what about informal and formal names for living things?

The wood louse is known in Britain by many local names - *tiggy-hog*, *cheeselog*, *pill bug*, *chiggy pig* and *rolypoly*, among others. Are these all to be counted as separate words? And, to take a more specialist example, is *saccharomyces cerevisiae*, the formal name for bread yeast, to be counted as a word (or perhaps as two)? If you say "yes", then you have to add another couple of million such names to the English language word count. And what about medical terms, such as *syncytiotrophoblastic* or *holoprosencephaly*, that few of us ever encounter?

THE COUNT FOR INDIVIDUALS

The other difficult term is *vocabulary*. What counts as a word that somebody knows? Is it one that a person uses regularly and accurately? Or perhaps one that will be correctly recognised - say in written text - but not used? Or perhaps one that will be understood in context, but which the person may not easily be able to define? This distinction between what linguists call active and passive vocabularies is hard to measure, and it skews estimates.

The problem doesn't stop there. English speakers not only know words, they know word-forming elements, such as the ending *-phobia* for some irrational fear. A journalist rushing to meet a deadline might take a word he knows, such as *Serb*, and tack on the ending to make *Serbophobia.* He's just added a word to the language (probably only temporarily), but can he really be said to have that word in his vocabulary? If nobody ever uses it again, can we legitimately count it? By reversing the coining process, a reader of the newspaper can easily work out the word's origin and meaning. Has the reader also added a word to his vocabulary?

Can you now see why estimates of the total number of words in the English language and in a person's vocabulary are so difficult to make, and why they vary so much one from another?

David Crystal, in the *Cambridge Encyclopedia of the English Language*, suggests that there must be at least a million words in the language. Tom McArthur, in the *Oxford Companion to the English Language*, comes up with a similar figure. David Crystal further says that if you allow all scientific terms then the total could easily reach two million (this doesn't count the formal names for organisms I spoke about earlier, just technical vocabulary).

Assessing the size of the vocabulary of an individual is at least as problematical. Take Shakespeare: one would think that it would be easy to assess his vocabulary. We have the plays and sonnets and we just have to count the words in them (according to the *American Heritage Dictionary*, there are 884,647 of them, made up of 29,066 distinct forms, including proper names). Estimates of Shakespeare's vocabulary vary from about 18,000 to 25,000 in various books, since writers have different views about what makes a word distinct.

It's common to see figures for vocabulary quoted such as 10,000 to 12,000 words for a 16-year-old, and 20,000 to 25,000 for a college graduate. These seem not to have much research to back them up. Usually they don't make clear whether active or passive vocabulary is being quoted, and they don't account for differences in lifestyle, profession and hobby interests between individuals.

David Crystal described a simple research project - using random pages from a dictionary - that suggests these figures are severe underestimates. He concludes that a better average for a college graduate might be 60,000 active words and 75,000 passive ones.

But this method of assessing vocabulary counts dictionary headwords only; it would be possible to multiply it several-fold to include different senses, inflected forms, and compounds. Another assessment – of a million-word collection of American texts – identified about 38,000 headwords. Bearing in mind that this was all general writing, this doesn't sound so different from David Crystal's estimates for graduate vocabularies.

CHAPTER 10

Established But Illogical Uses

Misquotations are the only quotations
that are never misquoted

- Hesketh Pearson

BACKGROUND

This chapter sets out certain words and expressions which are in common use despite really being quite illogical.

COMMONLY USED WORDS AND PHRASES

arguably. This word is often used as a synonym for "undoubtedly" - for example, "This is arguably the best value in town." However, the underlying meaning is "open to dispute or argument"; an arguable proposition is merely one for which a plausible case can be made out.

back to back. This expression, used in connection with two television programs screened in succession, would seem to call for two different words. Even metaphorically the back of the one program must touch the front (rather than the back) of the other.

billion, trillion. Originally these words were coined out of "bi-", two, and "tri-", three, in combination with "million". A billion was a million million and a trillion was a million million million - a coherent pattern. Unfortunately, a different, quite illogical, usage developed in the United States and France and has now taken over. Under this approach, a billion is 1000 million and a trillion is 1000 billion - see the Table at the end of this chapter. Because of this confusion, some people prefer to write "$3000 million" rather than risk an ambiguity by writing "$3 billion".

bit. "To take the bit between the teeth" is to be out of control or to rush headlong into something. The phrase does not mean to come to grips with the realities of a difficult problem. The appropriate metaphor for this is "to take the bull by the horns".

daylight saving time. Moving the clock forward does not alter the number of hours of daylight.

decimate. "To decimate" (to greatly reduce in size) is often used in the sense of "to reduce *to* one tenth", although its technical meaning is actually "to reduce *by* one tenth", in reference to executing every tenth soldier as the punishment for cowardice or mutiny.

hopefully. Technically, this is the adverb corresponding to the adjective "hopeful" and means "in a hopeful manner". However, it is also used as an adverb modifying a whole sentence, equivalent to "it is hoped {that}".

lowest common denominator. The mathematical term "*lowest* common denominator" is often used when actually speaking of the *highest* level of taste or the like found amongst all the members of some target audience.

milliard. See the Table at the end of this chapter.

near miss. This expression would more logically be "near hit"; it refers to an actual miss which was nearly a hit.

Parliament. A senior position in some Parliaments is called the "Clerk of the Parliaments". "Clerk of the Parliament", using that term in the singular, would be more logical - there is only one Parliament even if it happens to consist of two Houses.

present (and similar nouns). The same transaction can be rendered in two quite different ways:

> *Here is my present to you.*
>
> and
>
> *Here is your present from me.*

quantum leap. This metaphor is commonly used to mean "a giant step forward". In physics, the "leap" is actually extremely small (sub-atomic); however, the importance is the character rather than the size of the change.

revalue. In general usage this is a neutral term, implying a fresh valuation regardless of whether this results in a higher or lower figure; in relation to currency by convention the word "revalue" is not neutral and is used only for an upward movement - it is an antonym of "devalue".

tidal wave. An exceptionally huge ocean wave. It is usually caused by an earthquake and has no connection with the normal tides.

trillion. See the Table at the end of this chapter.

twenty-four hours. Statements such as those to the effect that something will happen "within twenty-four hours" do not mean that number of hours literally. Rather, they refer to the period ending either at midnight on the next day or at the close of business on the next day.

weekend. Traditionally a week is regarded as running from Sunday to Saturday inclusive. However, the term "weekend" is applied to the two-day period Saturday and the immediately following Sunday, thus really covering the beginning of the week as well as its end. The expression "long weekend" stretches this process even further, by including also the second day of the week, Monday, whenever this happens to be a public holiday.

HEIGHT AND WIDTH

Mathematicians, when plotting graphs, use what are known as Cartesian co-ordinates and always refer to the horizontal x-axis ahead of the vertical y-axis.

However, in the case of books and the like measurements are usually quoted the other way around - for example, 200 mm x 100 mm, being the height by the width. While the book and printing trades are no doubt used to this system it seems needlessly confusing to other persons.

TABLE

	Logical, Obsolete Version	Illogical, Current Version
10^{3}	thousand	thousand
10^{6}	million	million
10^{9}	milliard	billion
10^{12}	billion	trillion
10^{15}	billiard	
10^{18}	trillion	

CHAPTER 11

Metaphors Are Old Hat

Words are, of course, the most
powerful drug used by mankind

- Rudyard Kipling

WHAT IS A METAPHOR?

Many persons draw on similes, metaphors and other figures of speech to enrich their writing, usually without realising that they are doing this. Such expressions are often picturesque and help to convey meanings in relatively few words.

The author's Metaphors *(Bas Publishing, 2005) contains an overview of more than 4000 different metaphors in current circulation in English-speaking countries.*

The following extract from this 830-page book is included here as a matter of general interest. The passage was produced in answer to requests to name a few common metaphors.

Metaphors which have the community's seal of approval roll off the tongue so readily that, by any yardstick, they are invariably thick on the ground.

A person in the pink who plays his cards right and who takes up the cudgels for the cause will, without going overboard or changing tack, find an avalanche of metaphors under his very nose. Unless he puts a foot wrong or goes off half-cocked he will take the bull by the horns, bite the bullet, and regard them all as useful tools and as grist to his mill. He will already be in the picture and will not need to engage in a witchhunt or rely on the grapevine in order to put his finger on them.

Without matters getting out of hand or losing any momentum it stands out a mile that metaphors are in the blood of every Tom, Dick and Harry worth his salt and willing to show the flag.

Many expressions have been gathering dust for donkey's years and are so much a hallmark of our society that their down-to-earth use at the drop of a hat does not ring a bell or cause any eyebrows to be raised.

STATISTICS OF METAPHOR USAGE

Metaphors can be classified in various ways. One way is to have regard to the main subject area represented by the keyword in a metaphor.

The five largest of the categories in a representative sample of metaphors were as follows:

	CATEGORY	PERCENTAGE OF TOTAL
1	Human Body	21
2	Animals	8
3	Food and Drink	7
4	Farming	6
5	Sport	5

Such statistics have a fascination of their own - although admittedly their practical use is probably confined to being used as throw away lines in conversations over dinner and the like.

However, these figures do provide an interesting sociological commentary on the activities which most readily spring to mind when writers and speakers wish to make a point by using an analogy. In most cases the association will be readily understood by readers and listeners with a twenty-first century English speaking cultural background.

THE OTHER SIDE OF THE COIN

Do Investors Use Metaphors?

Financial journalists use colourful metaphors all the time - for example, share prices don't just go up or down - they either "skyrocket" or "go into a tailspin". Takeover offers are made "with much fanfare".

New chief executives "take the helm". Companies are either "in the black" or "in the red". Some groups make profits or losses large enough to be referred to as "telephone numbers".

Investors are perhaps more conscious of some other terms, as when they "burn their fingers" (lose money by foolish speculation) or when they are asked to "throw good money after bad" (waste further money in a vain attempt to recover their losses).

Little wonder that some of them prefer to "turn in their chips" (convert their assets into cash) after discovering that all investments are not "money for jam" (gains easily earned) and that some of their securities are no longer "above the water" (in excess of their cost price).

Brokers will know clients who try to "fly a kite" (issue uncovered cheques in the hope of covering them before clearance).

Commerce

Many expressions from the world of commerce have come into wider usage - for instance:

- "to be A1 at Lloyds" (to be in perfect order)
- "to give someone a blank cheque" (to give a person unlimited authority)
- "the other side of the coin" (the arguments for the opposite point of view)
- "to show dividends" (to be successful)

- "to be below par" (to be less than the desired standard)
- "a Rolls Royce solution" (a high quality but excessively expensive way of doing something)
- "it does not add up" (this does not make sense).

Political allusions to spending taxpayers' funds occur in expressions such as "to pork barrel" and "to engage in pump priming".

Money

The actual word "money" used in its literal sense is found in the partly-figurative phrases "to see the colour of someone's money", "to have money burning a hole in one's pocket", "putting one's money where one's mouth is", "money down the drain" and "the money is rolling in".

When a purely figurative expression for "money" is desired, words such as "pocket", "purse" or "penny" are often used, as in "to have deep pockets", "to line one's pocket", "to button up one's purse" and "to cost a pretty penny".

Sometimes colors are used in conjunction with the word "dollar" to convey particular ideas - for example:

- "pink dollars" (the profits generated from marketing goods and services to the homosexual community)
- "blue dollars" (the profits generated from the sale of soft pornography)
- "gray dollars" (the profits generated from marketing goods and services to older persons).

Mining and Oil

The price of gold does not always "go through the roof". However, investment in the mining and oil industry has led to a number of useful everyday metaphors, such as:

- "to pan out" (to succeed)

- "to stake a claim" (to indicate one's desire to obtain something)
- "to strike pay dirt" (to become successful)
- "a goldmine" (a source of much wealth or of many facts)
- "to get the good oil" (to receive useful, reliable and timely information).

Decimal Currency

Strange things happened when Australia's sterling currency was decimalised in 1966. Phrases such as "in for a penny, in for a pound", "the penny dropped", "a ha'p'orth of tar", "penny pinching" and the ungrammatical "he doesn't have two pennies to rub together" remained unchanged.

On the other hand, "to throw in one's six pennies' worth" became "to throw in one's two cents' worth", while "to have two bob each way" was converted to the version "to have fifty cents each way" - hardly close decimal equivalents.

Similarly, expressions involving imperial distances or weights do not always get metricated - for example:

- "to drain every ounce out of something"
- "to go the extra mile"
- "a yardstick"
- "a milestone"
- "not to give an inch"
- "to stand out a mile"
- "to get mileage out of some matter" and
- "to inch forward".

Of course, everyone with even 28.3 grams of common sense realises that exact conversions would not be appropriate in all circumstances.

GEORGE WASHINGTON QUIZ

A little bird once told me that modern Americans do not require the wisdom of Solomon to see the writing on the wall to the effect that they should kill the fatted calf and turn the other cheek, paying tribute to George Washington - the first President of the United States. He was no wolf in sheep's clothing, forced to wear a crown of thorns.

Not all Americans live in an ivory tower or want to raise Cain. Many managed well before the eleventh hour to be on the road to Damascus and thus to recognise a brilliant thinker who was the salt of the earth - a veritable Goliath well able both to put his hand to the plough and to cast his bread upon the waters.

Only a doubting Thomas would with a high hand fail to realise that Washington's efforts in founding a nation can indeed be used to separate the sheep from the goats. Reaching agreement on the Constitution of the United States was manna from heaven. The only fly in the ointment was that litigating all of its many features could try the patience of Job.

As with other great politicians, it can truly be said that by their fruits ye shall know them.

QUESTION: Just how many different expressions based on the Bible does the above passage contain?

ANSWER: 22, as follows:

a little bird once told me	Ecclesiastes 10:20
the wisdom of Solomon	1 Kings 3:16-28
the writing on the wall	Daniel 5
kill the fatted calf	Luke 15:23
turn the other cheek	Matthew 5:39
wolf in sheep's clothing	Matthew 7:15
to wear a crown of thorns	John 19:5
in an ivory tower	Song of Solomon 7:4
to raise Cain	Genesis 4:5
the eleventh hour	Matthew 20:9

to be on the road to Damascus	Acts 9:3
the salt of the earth	Matthew 5:13
a Goliath	1 Samuel 17
to put his hand to the plough	Luke 9:62
to cast his bread upon the waters	Ecclesiastes 11:1
a doubting Thomas	John 20:25
with a high hand	Exodus 14:8
to separate the sheep from the goats	Matthew 25:32
manna from heaven	Exodus 16:15
fly in the ointment	Ecclesiastes 10:1
the patience of Job	James 5:11
by their fruits ye shall know them	Matthew 7:20

GRASPING THE NETTLE WITH ELBOW GREASE

Politicians in our bailiwick who hop onto the bandwagon and line their own pockets have the cards stacked against them. Without letting the cat out of the bag it can be said off the cuff that they are on a sticky wicket and really need the wisdom of Solomon to stop the door closing on their activities.

They will have a hard row to hoe and, having burnt their bridges, will find themselves up a gum tree if they do not put their thinking caps on and plough on. Unless they can sharpen their axes or call the shots they will fail in their search for the Holy Grail and, while burning their fingers, will just sink deeper into the mire and become a footnote to history. This may not be a fair crack of the whip, but that is the way the cookie crumbles.

If, wanting a sea change but lacking a crystal ball, they bite the bullet and devise a scheme which kills the goose that lays the golden eggs then they will encounter road blocks and thus miss the boat.

The voters, keen to leave no stone unturned and having their fingers on the pulse, have sharpened their pencils and are now in the box seat. Used to fighting bushfires and keen to end the nightmare they will gnash their teeth, have kittens and seek fresh blood. The politicians will then not have a leg to stand on and will probably lose heart as they find themselves in hot water while rearranging the deckchairs on the Titanic.

However, life is no bed of roses and they must soldier on, grasping the nettle, ducking for cover and possibly engaging in some horse trading. The show has to go on and their colleagues - who all love fun and games and who are keen to strike the right note - will wish them the very best of British luck in their efforts to get out of the jam and batten down the hatches.

METAPHORS FROM THE BIBLE

The ancient non-Christian European religions gave rise to a number of current expressions, such as "to be in the lap of the gods" and "Delphic".

Primitive tribes in Africa originated the term "mumbo jumbo", while Australian aboriginal culture was the source of the expression "to point the bone at someone".

Both the Old and the New Testaments of the Bible contribute a surprisingly large number of phrases which are used by both believers and non-believers in circumstances far removed from those of their origin. Some of these phrases sound distinctly biblical, but many others do not.

Of course, the Bible in its English translation exists in many different editions. The classical expressions often come from the King James Version.

To illustrate, the Old Testament uses the oft-quoted "to hold out an olive branch", "the writing is on the wall", "to cast one's bread upon the waters" and "an eye for an eye, a tooth for a tooth". Somewhat surprisingly, the very modern term "to be in an ivory tower" also comes from this source.

Other Old Testament passages which give rise to currently-used expressions involve forbidden fruit, David and Goliath, the walls of Jericho, a fly in the ointment, the tower of Babel, the road to Damascus, the mark of Cain, feet of clay, manna from Heaven, the flesh pots of Egypt and the wisdom of Solomon.

"To sell one's birthright for a mess of pottage" (in other words, for a mere portion of soup) is another contemporary expression, although one which admittedly sounds rather quaint because of its archaic language.

The famous test word *shibboleth* has also passed into the language as the term for an out-dated political principle. (It is actually a Hebrew word meaning "stream in flood". Its significance in biblical times was that the way in which it was pronounced made it possible to tell an Ephraimite from a member of another tribe, because of his inability to pronounce the initial "sh" sound in some words correctly.)

The New Testament uses the popular "by their fruits ye shall know them" and refers to a wolf in sheep's clothing, the salt of the earth, putting one's hand to the plough, turning the other cheek, killing the fatted calf, being a doubting Thomas, separating the sheep from the goats, being a good Samaritan and seeing the mote in another person's eye.

EXAMPLES OF BIBLICAL METAPHORS

A small sample of biblical metaphors (in alphabetical order of the keywords) is set out below:

ASHES - to wear sackcloth and ashes = humbly to demonstrate repentance (Esther 4:3)

BABE - out of the mouths of babes and sucklings = (as indiscreetly revealed) the truth (Psalms 8:2)

BABEL - a tower of Babel = a noisy and confused assembly (Genesis 11)

BEAR - to be a cross which one has to bear = to be a difficulty which one has to endure (Luke 14:27)

BIRD - a little bird told me = I heard from an unnamable informant (Ecclesiastes 10:20)

BIRTHRIGHT - to sell one's birthright for a mess of pottage = through foolishness to exchange something of substance for something of little value (Genesis 25)

BLIND - the blind leading the blind = persons without the necessary skills for a task purporting to impart those skills to others (Matthew 15:14)

BREAD - to cast one's bread upon the waters = not to expect gratitude or recognition for one's good works (Ecclesiastes 11:1)

BUSHEL - to hide one's light under a bushel = to keep others in ignorance of one's skills and experience (Luke 11:33)

CAIN - the mark of Cain = disgrace (Genesis 4:15)

CAIN - to raise Cain = to create a disturbance (Genesis 4:5)

CALF - to kill the fatted calf = to demonstrate welcome and forgiveness on a person's return (Luke 15:23)

CAST - to cast one's bread upon the waters = not to expect gratitude or recognition for one's good works (Ecclesiastes 11:1)

CHAFF - to separate the wheat from the chaff = to distinguish between important and unimportant ingredients (Luke 3:17)

CHEEK - to turn the other cheek = to show that one has not been intimidated (Matthew 5:39)

CLAY - to have feet of clay = to be vulnerable or not as good as thought (Daniel 2:33)

CLOTHING - to be a wolf in sheep's clothing = to be a hypocrite or to be dangerous although masquerading as something harmless (Matthew 7:15)

CROSS - to be a cross which one has to bear = to be a difficulty which one has to endure (Luke 14:27)

CROWN - to wear one's crown of thorns = to have one's own difficulties (John 19:5)

CRUCIFY - to crucify someone = to unfairly do severe damage to a person's reputation or credibility (Mark 15:13)

DAMASCUS - to be on the road to Damascus = to see the error of one's ways (Acts 9:3)

DAVID - a David and Goliath battle = a struggle between two parties who are not evenly matched (1 Samuel 17:23)

DOUBT - a doubting Thomas = a person who refuses to believe claims in the absence of proof (John 20:25)

EARTH - to be the salt of the earth = to be a person whose ordinary efforts benefit the community (Matthew 5:13)

EDGE - to be a two-edged sword = to involve both advantages and disadvantages of similar significance (Psalms 149:6)

ELEVEN - at the eleventh hour = at the last moment (actually 'at the twenty-fourth hour' would be more logical) (Matthew 20:9)

EYE - a mote in someone's eye = a fault in another person which is trifling in comparison to an unrecognised major fault in oneself (Matthew 7:3)

EYE - an eye for an eye = retaliation (Exodus 21:24)

FLESHPOT - fleshpots = sumptuous living (Exodus 16:3)

FLY - a fly in the ointment = a flaw (refers to dead flies turning perfumes rancid) (Ecclesiastes 10:1)

FOOT - to have feet of clay = to be vulnerable or not as good as thought (Daniel 2:33)

FORBID - forbidden fruit = something particularly desired just because it is not allowed (Genesis 2:17)

FRUIT - by their fruits ye shall know them = their reputation will be based on their results (Matthew 7:20)

FRUIT - forbidden fruit = something particularly desired just because it is not allowed (Genesis 2:17)

GOAT - to separate the sheep from the goats = to distinguish between those with and without certain attributes (Matthew 25:32)

GOLIATH - a David and Goliath battle = a struggle between two parties who are not evenly matched (1 Samuel 17:23)

GOLIATH - a Goliath = a giant (1 Samuel 17:23)

GOLIATH - a Goliath = a giant or a person whose ability and achievements exceed that of most other people (1 Samuel 17)

GOMORRAH - a Sodom and Gomorrah = a place of vice (Genesis 18:20)

HAND - the left hand does not know what the right hand is doing = one section of a large bureaucracy does not realise that another section is simultaneously doing something inconsistent (Matthew 6:3)

HAND - to put one's hand to the plough = voluntarily to undertake some task (Luke 9:62)

HAND - with a high hand = arrogantly (Exodus 14:8)

HEAVEN - manna from heaven = unexpected benefits (Exodus 16:15)

HIDE - to hide one's light under a bushel = to keep others in ignorance of one's skills and experience (Luke 11:33)

HIGH - with a high hand = arrogantly (Exodus 14:8)

HONEY - a land of milk and honey = a country in which everything is in abundant supply (Exodus 3:8)

HOUR - at the eleventh hour = at the last moment (actually 'at the twenty-fourth hour' would be more logical) (Matthew 20:9)

IRON - to rule with a rod of iron = to keep strict discipline (Psalms 52:9)

IVORY - to be in an ivory tower = to be emersed in theoretical considerations and ignorant of the practical realities (Song of Solomon 7:4)

JEREMIAH - Jeremiah = a person who looks on the gloomy side of everything (refers to the prophet Jeremiah in the Old Testament)

JERICHO - walls of Jericho = something seemingly solid but actually destructible (Joshua 6:20)

JEZEBEL - a Jezebel = a shameless woman (1 Kings 16:31)

JOB - something would try the patience of Job = something is very vexatious (James 5:11)

JUDAS - to play Judas = to betray a person (Matthew 26)

KILL - to kill the fatted calf = to demonstrate welcome and forgiveness on a person's return (Luke 15:23)

KNOW - by their fruits ye shall know them = their reputation will be based on their results (Matthew 7:20)

LEFT - the left hand does not know what the right hand is doing = one section of a large bureaucracy does not realise that another section is simultaneously doing something inconsistent (Matthew 6:3)

LIGHT - to hide one's light under a bushel = to keep others in ignorance of one's skills and experience (Luke 11:33)

LIGHT - to see the light = to understand the real situation (Luke 8:16)

LITTLE - a little bird told me = I heard from an unnamable informant (Ecclesiastes 10:20)

MANNA - manna from heaven = unexpected benefits (Exodus 16:15)

MARK - the mark of Cain = disgrace (Genesis 4:15)

MESS - to sell one's birthright for a mess of pottage = through foolishness to exchange something of substance for something of little value (Genesis 25)

MILK - a land of milk and honey = a country in which everything is in abundant supply (Exodus 3:8)

MOTE - a mote in someone's eye = a fault in another person which is trifling in comparison to an unrecognised major fault in oneself (Matthew 7:3)

MOUTH - out of the mouths of babes and sucklings = (as indiscreetly revealed) the truth (Psalms 8:2)

OINTMENT - a fly in the ointment = a flaw (refers to dead flies turning perfumes rancid) (Ecclesiastes 10:1)

OLIVE - to hold out an olive branch = to make peace overtures (Genesis 8:11)

PATIENCE - something would try the patience of Job = something is very vexatious (James 5:11)

PLOUGH - to put one's hand to the plough = voluntarily to undertake some task (Luke 9:62)

POT - fleshpots = sumptuous living (Exodus 16:3)

POTTAGE - to sell one's birthright for a mess of pottage = through foolishness to exchange something of substance for something of little value (Genesis 25)

RAISE - to raise Cain = to create a disturbance (Genesis 4:5)

RIGHT - the left hand does not know what the right hand is doing = one section of a large bureaucracy does not realise that another section is simultaneously doing something inconsistent (Matthew 6:3)

ROAD - to be on the road to Damascus = to see the error of one's ways (Acts 9:3)

ROD - to rule with a rod of iron = to keep strict discipline (Psalms 52:9)

SACKCLOTH - to wear sackcloth and ashes = humbly to demonstrate repentance (Esther 4:3)

SALT - to be the salt of the earth = to be a person whose ordinary efforts benefit the community (Matthew 5:13)

SAMARITAN - a good Samaritan = a person going out of his way to do a kindness to others (Luke 10:33)

SCAPEGOAT - a scapegoat = a person unfairly blamed for something not his fault (Leviticus 16:10)

SELL - to sell one's birthright for a mess of pottage = through foolishness to exchange something of substance for something of little value (Genesis 25)

SEPARATE - to separate the sheep from the goats = to distinguish between those with and without certain attributes (Matthew 25:32)

SHEEP - to be a wolf in sheep's clothing = to be a hypocrite or to be dangerous although masquerading as something harmless (Matthew 7:15)

SHEEP - to separate the sheep from the goats = to distinguish between those with and without certain attributes (Matthew 25:32)

SHIBBOLETH - a shibboleth = a doctrine once held as essential but now abandoned as having outlived its usefulness (a word used as a test to determine to which tribe an Israelite belonged) (Judges 12:6)

SKIN - to escape by the skin of one's teeth = to only just avoid some disaster (Job 19:20)

SODOM - a Sodom and Gomorrah = a place of vice (Genesis 18:20)

SOLOMON - to need the wisdom of Solomon = to be faced with the need to make a difficult decision (1 Kings 3:16-28)

SONG - to be in an ivory tower = to be emersed in theoretical considerations and ignorant of the practical realities (Song of Solomon 7:4)

SUCKLING - out of the mouths of babes and sucklings = (as indiscreetly revealed) the truth (Psalms 8:2)

SWORD - to be a two-edged sword = to involve both advantages and disadvantages of similar significance (Psalms 149:6)

THOMAS - a doubting Thomas = a person who refuses to believe claims in the absence of proof (John 20:25)

THORN - to wear one's crown of thorns = to have one's own difficulties (John 19:5)

TOOTH - a tooth for a tooth = retaliation (Exodus 21:24)

TOOTH - to escape by the skin of one's teeth = to only just avoid some disaster (Job 19:20)

TOWER - to be in an ivory tower = to be emersed in theoretical considerations and ignorant of the practical realities (Song of Solomon 7:4)

TRY - something would try the patience of Job = something is very vexatious (James 5:11)

TURN - to turn the other cheek = to show that one has not been intimidated (Matthew 5:39)

TWO - to be a two-edged sword = to involve both advantages and disadvantages of similar significance (Psalms 149:6)

WALL - to see the writing on the wall = to appreciate the inevitability of some event (Daniel 5)

WALL - walls of Jericho = something seemingly solid but actually destructible (Joshua 6:20)

WATER - to cast one's bread upon the waters = not to expect gratitude or recognition for one's good works (Ecclesiastes 11:1)

WEAR - to wear one's crown of thorns = to have one's own difficulties (John 19:5)

WHEAT - to separate the wheat from the chaff = to distinguish between important and unimportant ingredients (Luke 3:17)

WILDERNESS - to be in the wilderness = to be out of office against one's will (Numbers 14:33)

WISDOM - to need the wisdom of Solomon = to be faced with the need to make a difficult decision (1 Kings 3:16-28)

WOLF - to be a wolf in sheep's clothing = to be a hypocrite or to be dangerous although masquerading as something harmless (Matthew 7:15)

WRITE - to see the writing on the wall = to appreciate the inevitability of some event (Daniel 5)

CHAPTER 12

Assorted Lists

The only English word starting with "mn-" is "mnemonic" - and don't you forget it

USEFUL MNEMONICS

Mnemonic for the nine planets in order - Mercury, Venus, Earth, Mars, Jupiter, Saturn, Uranus, Neptune, Pluto:

My very earnest mother just showed us nine planets.

Mnemonic for the seven colours of the rainbow in order - Red, Orange, Yellow, Green, Blue, Indigo, Violet:

Richard of York gained battles in vain.

STRANGE NEWSPAPER HEADLINES

The *Age*, discussing a predicted decline in housing commencements, used the rather misleading headline: "House Starts to Fall."

Some other examples from various parts of the globe are as follows:

Squad Helps Dog Bite Victim

Miners Refuse to Work after Death

March Planned for next August

Blind Bishop Appointed to See

Patient at Death's Door - Doctors Pull Him Through

Defendant's Speech Ends in Long Sentences

Two Sisters Reunited after 18 Years in Checkout Counter

Typhoon Rips through Cemetery - Hundreds Dead

Lingerie Shipment Hijacked - Thief Gives Police the Slip

Community Bands Together to Help Burn Victim's Family

Something Went Wrong in Jet Crash, Expert Says

Prostitutes Appeal to Pope

Juvenile Court to Try Shooting Defendant

New Study of Obesity Looks for Larger Test Group

Kids Make Nutritious Snacks

Bald Men's Club Offers Chance to Let Hair Down

Girlie Mags must Stay Abreast of the Net

SOME TIPS FOR NEW WRITERS

Never use a long word when a diminutive one will do.

Clichés are old hat - avoid them like the plague.

Eschew ampersands & abbreviations, etc.

Parenthetical remarks (however relevant) are best avoided.

Remember to never split an infinitive.

Foreign words and phrases are not apropos.

One should never generalise.

Comparisons are as bad as clichés.

Be more or less specific.

One-word sentences? Eliminate.

Analogies in writing are like feathers on a snake.

The passive voice is to be avoided.

Go around the barn at high noon to avoid colloquialisms.

Even if a mixed metaphor sings, it should be derailed.

Who needs rhetorical questions?

Exaggeration is a billion times worse than understatement.

Don't never use a double negation.

capitalise the first word of every sentence.

End every sentence with a full stop

Do not put statements in the negative form.

Verbs has to agree with their subjects.

Proofread carefully to see if you words out.

And don't start a sentence with a conjunction.

A preposition is a terrible word to end a sentence with.

Don't overuse exclamation marks!!!

Writing carefully, dangling participles must be avoided.

Take the bull by the hand and avoid mixing metaphors.

Don't be redundant; don't use more words than necessary; that would be highly superfluous.

NEW OLYMPIC EVENTS

Beating around the bush

Jumping to conclusions

Climbing the walls

Swallowing your pride

Passing the buck

Throwing your weight around

Dragging your heels

Pushing your luck

Making mountains out of molehills

Hitting the nail on the head

Wading through paperwork

Bending over backwards
Jumping on the bandwagon
Balancing the books
Running around in circles
Eating crow
Tooting your own horn
Climbing the ladder of success
Pulling out all the stops
Adding fuel to the fire
Opening a can of worms
Putting your foot in your mouth
Starting the ball rolling
Going over the edge
Picking up the pieces

HOW TO CONFUSE FOREIGNERS

He could lead if he would get the lead out.
The farm was used to produce produce.
The dump was so full that it had to refuse more refuse.
The soldier decided to desert in the desert.
This was a good time to present the present.
When shot at, the dove dove into the bushes.
I did not object to the object.
The insurance was invalid for the invalid.
The bandage was wound around the wound.
There was a row among the oarsmen about how to row.
They were too close to the door to close it.
The buck does funny things when the does are present.
They sent a sewer down to stitch the tear in the sewer line.
To help with planting, the farmer taught his sow to sow.

The wind was too strong to wind the sail.

After a number of injections my jaw got number.

Upon seeing the tear in my clothes I shed a tear.

I had to subject the subject to a series of tests.

How can I intimate this to my most intimate friend?

The fisherman painted a picture of a bass on the head of the bass drum.

We must polish the Polish furniture.

DID YOU KNOW ...?

That there is no egg in an eggplant?

That there is no ham in a hamburger?

That there is neither pine nor apple in a pineapple?

That English muffins were not invented in England?

That French fries were not invented in France?

That quicksand actually drags people down slowly?

That boxing rings are square?

That a guinea pig is neither from Guinea nor is it a pig?

That people recite at a play yet play at a recital?

That when the stars are out they are visible but when the lights are out they are invisible?

That sweetmeats are candies while sweetbreads, which do not taste sweet, are meat.

That people have noses that run and feet that smell?

That a slim chance and a fat chance are the same, while a wise man and a wise guy are opposites?

That the English horn is neither English nor a horn? (It was developed in France, like the oboe, and is technically a woodwind. The word "horn" is properly applied only to brass instruments.)

ANNIVERSARIES

Year	Name
1	paper
2	cotton
3	leather
4	linen
5	wood
6	iron
7	wool
8	bronze
9	pottery
10	aluminum
11	steel
12	silk
13	lace
14	ivory
15	crystal
20	china
25	silver
30	pearl
35	coral
40	ruby
45	sapphire
50	gold
55	emerald
60	diamond

HYBRID ANIMALS

An animal which is the offspring of a male animal of one species and a female animal of another is known as a *crossbreed* or *hybrid animal.* In many cases such animals are also referred to by hybrid names such as in the examples below. The convention with most such names is that the male animal contributes the first half of the word and the female the second half.

Hybrid	Male Parent	Female Parent
liger	male lion	female tiger
tigon	male tiger	female lion
mule	male donkey	mare
hinny	male horse	female donkey
beefalo	male bison	cow
zeedonk	male zebra	female donkey
zorse	male zebra	female horse
wholphin	male whale	female dolphin

STOLEN BY COMPUTER GEEKS

The computer industry has taken numerous ordinary English words and given them special meanings. The best-known ones include the following:

bandwidth
bit
boot
browser
bug
card
chip
client
cookie
disk
drive
environment
fingerprint
firewall
flag

frames

gateway

handshake

hardware

heartbeat

host

icon

master and slave

memory

menu

mirror

mouse

packet

patch

path

payload

portal

proxy

sandbox

server

site

software

surfing

syntax

Trojan horse

virus

web

wild card

window

word

worm

THE MOST WIDELY SPOKEN LANGUAGES IN THE WORLD

Language	Approximate Number of Speakers (million)
1. Chinese (Mandarin)	1,075
2. English	514
3. Hindustani	496
4. Spanish	425
5. Russian	275
6. Arabic	256
7. Bengali	215
8. Portuguese	194
9. Malay-Indonesian	176
10. Japanese	125

These figures refer to first language speakers in all countries. They are broad estimates only. Different authorities produce vastly different figures for this subject, because of different definitions and because of the practical difficulties in the enumeration process.

HOW MANY LANGUAGES ARE THERE?

The number of languages in the world, according to the *Ethnologue* (15th edition, 2005), is 6,912. Once again, different definitions are possible and this figure is only one of several estimates which have been published.

For more details, see

http://www.ethnologue.com/ethno_docs/distribution.asp?by=area

OFFICIAL LANGUAGES

Despite the numerous languages of its member states the United Nations Organisation has only six official languages:

1. the four languages of the five nations which founded the UNO:
   - Chinese
   - English
   - French
   - Russian
2. two languages added later on, because they are widely spoken:
   - Arabic
   - Spanish

In contrast, all 20 languages spoken by the 25 members of the European Union are official languages of that body:

Language	ISO 639-1 Code
Czech	cs
Danish	da
Dutch	nl
English	en
Estonian	et
Finnish	fi
French	fr
German	de
Greek	el
Hungarian	hu
Italian	it
Latvian	lv
Lithuanian	lt
Maltese	mt
Polish	pl

Language	ISO 639-1 Code
Portuguese	pt
Slovak	sk
Slovene	sl
Spanish	es
Swedish	sv

ACRONYMS

Acronyms are words artificially coined from the initial (and possibly further) letters of other words. Long-established ones include:

- Anzac (originally "Australian and New Zealand Army Corps")
- laser (originally "Light Amplification by Stimulated Emission of Radiation")
- qango (originally "Quasi-Autonomous National Government Organisation")
- Qantas (originally "Queensland and Northern Territory Aerial Services")
- radar (originally "RAdio Detecting And Ranging").

A good web site for looking up acronyms is

http://www.acronymfinder.com

although it has a mild United States bias.

Sometimes entertaining stories are made up to explain names which are not really acronyms - for example, TWAIN, which is variously said to stand for "Technology Without An Interesting Name" or "Toolkit Without An Important Name" or other similar combinations. (TWAIN is a widely used computer program that lets users use a scanner in order to scan an image directly into an application which enables them to work on that image.)

Social organisations often choose light-hearted or humorous or self-mocking names for themselves - for example:

- ASH (a body called "Action on Smoking and Health")
- BUGAUP (a body called "Billboard Utilising Graffitists Against Unhealthy Products")
- PLACE (a body called "People, Landscape, Art, Conservation and Environment")
- SHARE (a body called "Self Help Association through Responsibility and Enrichment")
- WIRE (a body called "Women's Information and Referral Exchange")

Other recent frivolous acronyms include:

- DEAR ("Drop Everything And Read")
- FIFO ("Fit In or Fuck Off"; with apologies to accountants, who think that it just means "First In, First Out")
- GIGO (a computer term meaning "Garbage In, Garbage Out")
- LOMBARD ("Lots Of Money, But A Real Dickhead")
- MABO ("Money Available, Barristers Only", in reference to the native title litigation fought in the name of Eddie Mabo)
- SAUA (a hypothetical organisation called the "Society Against the Use of Abbreviations")
- SOB ("short of breath")

There are even stories dealing with the word ACRONYM itself - for example:

> A Cunning Reminder Of a Name You Misplaced
>
> Australian Campaign to Reduce Overly Noxious Yankee Mimicry

And, then, of course, one can even refer to a TLA (a Three-Letter Acronym).

BUZZ WORDS

Persons who wish to put impressive sounding phrases into reports that they are producing can generate 1,000 such expressions from the table below. The method is to choose at random one word from each of the three columns in order - for example, "systemised transitional projection". Readers of such reports will not be able to make sense of such nonsense phrases, but they may not wish to admit this.

Column 1	Column 2	Column 3
integrated	management	options
total	organisational	flexibility
systemised	monitored	capability
parallel	reciprocal	mobility
functional	digital	programming
responsive	logic	concept
optical	transitional	time phase
synchronised	incremental	projection
compatible	third generation	hardware
balanced	policy	contingency

A much more elaborate electronic version of this buzzword generators is available at

http://www.1728.com/buzzword.htm

This can produce 1,050,400 different phrases at random.

CHAPTER 13

Some Curiosities Of The English Language

If you think education is expensive, try ignorance

- anon

"OUGH"

The combination "ough" can be pronounced in eight different ways. The following sentence contains them all:

A rough-coated, dough-faced ploughman strode through the streets of Scarborough, coughing and hiccoughing thoughtfully.

VOWELS

Some words contain the five vowels in the correct order, including three consecutively - for example:

abstemious, arsenious, facetious.

The shortest word of this type is *aerious.*

Some words which contain them in the reverse order are:

subcontinental, uncomplimentary, unnoticeably.

The longest word (nine letters) containing only one vowel is *strengths.*

The word *defencelessness* uses only one of the five vowels, "e", but contains it five times.

The word *indivisibilities* contains the vowel "i" seven times.

CONSONANTS

A small number of words contain four consecutive consonants (treating a pronounced "y" as a vowel for this purpose). These include:

> *diphtheria, diphthong, isthmus, phthisis,* as well as
> *fourthly*, and so on.

The word *eighthly* even contains five consecutive consonants (or six, if the "y" is included).

The word *phenolphthalein* also contains five consecutive consonants.

The words *latchstring* and *catchphrase* contains six consecutive consonants.

The word *rhythms* contains seven consecutive consonants (including "y") but not a single vowel.

CONSECUTIVE WORDS

The following sentence contains the word "and" five times consecutively:

> *In the sign reading "Coach and Horses" there is too much space between "Coach" and "and" and "and" and "Horses".*

The following sentence contains the word "that" seven times consecutively:

> *I know that: that that "that" that that "that" followed was ungrammatical.*

The following sentence contains the word "had" 11 times consecutively:

> *Tom, where John had had "had", had had "had had"; "had had" had had the inspector's approval.*

SOME PUZZLES

- "Fred sows. Mary sews. Both s-w."

What is the missing letter?

- Can you think of a word with three *u*'s?

Hint: The word is unusual!

- Is there a word which uses all vowels including "y"?

Unquestionably.

- What is said to be the toughest tongue twister in the English language?

"The sixth sick sheik's sixth sheep's sick."

ALPHABET SOUP

A voter who objected to a political proposal claimed to be annoyed, bristling, cross, displeased, enraged, furious, galled, horrified, irritated, jarred, kayoed, lachrymose, miserable, nauseated, offended, piqued, querulous, rancorous, sickened, testy, upset, vengeful, wrathful, xenophobic, yammering and zestless.

THE SHORTEST PANGRAM

A *pangram* is a sentence which uses all 26 letters of the alphabet. The shortest pangram which does not involve a proper noun is:

Sphinx of black quartz, judge my vow.

It contains 29 letters; a, o and u are used twice, every other letter is used only once.

The classic sentence which contains every letter of the alphabet is:

The quick brown fox jumps over the lazy dog.

TWO INTERESTING ANAGRAMS

To be or not to be: that is the question, whether 'tis nobler in the mind to suffer the slings and arrows of outrageous fortune.

In one of the Bard's best-thought-of tragedies, our insistent hero, Hamlet, queries on two fronts about how life turns rotten.

President Clinton of the USA.

To copulate he finds interns.

THE LONGEST WORD

The longest word listed in a non-specialist English dictionary is

pneumonoultramicroscopicsilicovolcanoconiosis.

This 45-letter word means a respiratory condition caused by very fine mineral particles, such as might be generated by an erupting volcano.

The longest word in which no letter occurs only once is

unprosperousness.

The longest one-syllable word is

screeched.

However, the word with the longest definition in most dictionaries is actually quite short:

set

A rather weird word is

artiformologicalintactitudinarianisminist

a person who studies Latin prefixes and suffixes.

CONTRANYMS

A *contranym* or *contronym* or *antagonym* is a word having two opposite meanings:

citation: words relating to an award for good behavior

citation: words relating to a penalty for bad behavior

cleave: to come apart

cleave: to adhere

dust: to remove dust

dust: to sprinkle with dust (as when taking fingerprints)

fast: moving quickly

fast: staying fixed in position

left: remaining

left: having departed

let: hinder

let: allow

lift a levy: to increase the rate of levy

lift a levy: to abolish a levy

moot: arguable

moot: not worthy of argument

oversight: watchful control

oversight: a failure to notice

sanction: to permit

sanction: to impose a penalty

PREFIXES AND SUFFIXES

The word with the most prefixes and suffixes (five) is *incomprehensibility*.

A WORD WITH THREE APOSTROPHES

fo'c's'le

DOUBLE AND TREBLE LETTERS

Words with three consecutive pairs of double letters include

bookkeeper, bookkeeping.

A word with four consecutive pairs of double letters is

subbookkeeper.

The only word with a treble letter is

goddessship.

LETTERS IN ALPHABETICAL ORDER

The following are examples of words containing three consecutive letters in alphabetical order:

- DEF defined
- HIJ hijinks
- NOP monopoly
- RST thirst
- STU astute

UNREPEATABLE

The only 15-letter word that can be spelt without repeating a letter is *uncopyrightable.*

TYPEWRITER TRIVIA

The word *typewriter* can be typed using only the top line of a typewriter keyboard.

The longest words in common use which can be typed with only the left hand include:

stewardesses and *reverbarated* (12 letters each).

The longest such words which can be typed with only the right hand include:

lollipop and *monopoly.*

The longest such word which can be typed with both hands alternately is *skepticism.*

"REFLEXIVE ONLY" VERBS

The following verbs can be used only in reflexive constructions:

to perjure oneself
to absent oneself (from something)
to pride oneself (on something)

DOUBLETS AND TRIPLETS

The terms *doublets* and *triplets* refer to phrases containing unnecessary synonyms. They are often found in legal documents and in works such as the *Book of Common Prayer.* The following are examples:

acknowledge and confess
act and deed
agree and covenant
aims and objects
alms and oblations
any and all

bag and baggage
beg and beseech
cancel, annul and set aside
cease and desist
create and make
due and owing
fears and apprehensions
first and foremost
fit and proper
force and effect
give, devise and bequeath
goods and chattels
have and hold
in my stead and place
keep and maintain
let and hindrance
made and signed
neat and tidy
null and void
object and purpose
one and only
order and direct
ordered and adjudged
pale and wan
pardon, remission and absolution
pay, satisfy and discharge
perform and discharge
pray and beseech
rest, residue and remainder
terms and conditions
will and testament

The sequence of words in "ordered and adjudged" seems curious. In practice a court would adjudicate a matter before deciding on any orders it should make.

HOW TO SPELL "EE"

To the confusion of foreigners the "ee" sound as in "bee" or "sleep" can be spelt in at least 10 different ways in English, as follows:

Spelling	Example
e	be
ea	sea
ee	see
ei	receive
eo	people
ey	key
i	police
ie	believe
is	debris
uay	quay

"GHOTI"

Q. What does the word "ghoti" spell?

A. "fish".

"gh" as in "enouGH"
"o" as in "wOmen"
"ti" as in "staTIon"

SMOKING

A clever advertisement depicted a female athlete ahead of the field in a footrace.

The slogan read:

You won't catch her smoking.

THE UNITED STATES CONSTITUTION

In recent years there have been vigorous arguments in the United States between those for and against gun controls. Such discussions often refer to the Second Amendment to the United States Constitution, which reads as follows:

> "Amendment II
>
> A well regulated Militia, being necessary to the security of a free State, the right of the people to keep and bear Arms, shall not be infringed."

It will be noticed that the first and third commas in this clause do not make grammatical sense and that three capitalised words ought to be rendered in lower case.

As these commas and capitals do not occur in some reprints of the Constitution the author wrote to the Historian of the United States Senate in Washington DC to ask what the official version enacted in 1791 really was.

Her disappointing reply made three points:

- That, not being a constitutional scholar, she was not able the answer. However, the question related to a historical fact, not to a constitutional aspect.
- That this matter should be checked out in "your local library". Wonderful as some of these institutions are in Australia they are unlikely to be strong on such esoteric foreign historical material.
- That copies of the Constitution could be found in various textbooks and on various web sites which she named. But the reason for writing in the first place was that these secondary sources showed different versions and that what was really required was information about the *original* document.

The author, being a perfectionist, then tried again and eventually tracked down another expert in Washington, Dr Milton Gustafson, Archivist, Textual Archives Services Division of the United States National Archives and Records Administration, who advised as follows:

* * *

> Number of Commas and Capitalization in the Bill of Rights, Second Amendment: The Right to Keep and Bear Arms
>
> The following information is taken from *Amendments to the Constitution, A Brief Legislative History, Committee Print, 99th Congress, 1st Session (S. Prt. 99-87), Washington: U.S. Government Printing Office, 1985.*
>
> The following version, part of a Bill of Rights containing 17 Amendments, was approved by the House of Representatives on August 24, 1789, and sent to the Senate:
>
> "ART. V. A well regulated militia, composed of the body of the people, being the best security of a free state, the right of the people to keep and bear arms shall not be infringed, but no one relgiously *sic* scrupulous of bearing arms shall be compelled to render military service in person."
>
> The Senate reduced the number of Amendments to 12, with a shortened version:
>
> "ART. IV. A well regulated militia being necessary to the security of a free state, the right of the people to keep and bear arms shall not be infringed."
>
> On September 26, 1789, Congress passed a joint resolution, signed by the President of the Senate and the Speaker of the House, and sent copies of it to the States for ratification. This version, the only signed copy, is on display in the National Archives Building. The text is as follows:

> "Article the fourth. A well regulated Militia, being necessary to the security of a free State, the right of the people to keep and bear Arms, shall not be infringed."
>
> Some publications contain the version of the 2nd Amendment as approved by the Senate, with only one comma, but the official version is the joint resolution approved by both Houses of Congress, signed by John Adams and Frederick Augustus Muhlenberg, the one with three commas and capitalized Militia, State, and Arms.

* * *

So there we have it. The grammatical version drafted by the United States Senate got mangled on its way through the subsequent stages. Some publishers of the Constitution favoured good grammar, while others went for historical accuracy. And what about the members of the NRA - the National Rifle Association - and its opponents? Like the rest of the nation they probably did not notice and, even if they did, did not really care one way or the other. Sic transit gloria mundi.

THE CAMBRIDGE EXPERIMENT

cehck tihs out:

> Aoccdrnig to a rseerach at Cmabrigde Uinervtisy, it deosn't mttaer in waht oredr the ltteers in a wrod are, the olny iprmoetnt tihng is taht the frist and lsat ltteer be at the rghit pclae.
>
> The rset can be a total mses and you can sitll raed it wouthit porbelm. Tihs is bcuseae the huamn mnid deos not raed ervey lteter by istlef, but the wrod as a wlohe. Amzanig, huh?

Notes:

- The earliest example of this passage on the Internet appears to date from 13 September 2003.
- While this material is clearly very clever, the research aspect is probably a hoax. See

http://www.snopes.com/language/apocryph/cambridge.asp

- A Google search on "bcuseae" shortly after this item first surfaced showed that at least 120,000 web pages were then carrying some version or other of this story - and no doubt numerous e-mails have also reproduced it. The speed of this happening was remarkable.

THE LONGEST LIPOGRAM

A *lipogram* is a work of writing that deliberately excludes one or more particular letters. The longest lipogram in the English language is *Gadsby*, a novel by the American writer Ernest Vincent Wright (1872-1939). It contains 50,110 words without using the letter *E*. This precluded the use of common words such as *the*.

In his introduction the author says that his entire manuscript was written with the *E* type-bar of his typewriter tied down, thus making it impossible for that letter to be printed. This was done so that none of that vowel might slip in accidentally.

The following is an edited version of the introduction:

> "In writing such a story, purposely avoiding all words containing the vowel *E*, there are a great many difficulties. The greatest of these is met in the past tense of verbs, almost all of which end with *-ed*. Therefore substitutes must be found; and they are very few. This will cause, at times, a somewhat monotonous use of such words as *said*; for neither *replied*, *answered* nor *asked* can be used.
>
> "Another difficulty comes with the elimination of the common couplet *of course*, and its very common connective, *consequently*; which will unavoidably cause bumpy spots. The numerals also cause plenty of trouble, for none between six and thirty are available. When introducing young ladies into the story, this is a real barrier; for what young woman wants to have it known

> that she is over thirty? And this restriction on numbers, of course, taboos all mention of dates.
>
> "Many abbreviations also must be avoided; the most common of all, *Mr* and *Mrs* being particularly troublesome; for those words, if read aloud, plainly indicate the *E* in their orthography.
>
> "As the vowel *E* is used more than five times as often as any other letter, this story was written, not through any attempt to attain literary merit, but due to a somewhat balky nature, caused by hearing it so constantly claimed that it can't be done.
>
> "Many may think that I simply dropped the *E*s, filling the gaps with apostrophes. A perusal of the book will show that this is not so. All words used are complete; are correctly spelled and properly used. This has been accomplished through the use of synonyms, and by so twisting a sentence around as to avoid ambiguity.
>
> "Pronouns also caused trouble; for such words as *he, she, they, them, theirs, her, herself, myself, himself, yourself,* etc., could not be utilised."

The full text of the novel, which is now out of copyright, is online at

http://www.spinelessbooks.com/gadsby/

LOREM IPSUM

Lorem Ipsum is the standard dummy text of the printing and typesetting industry. It is used to stop readers becoming distracted by the readable content of a page when looking at its layout.

Lorem Ipsum is a Latin passage which has a more-or-less normal distribution of letters, thus making it look like readable English:

> *Lorem ipsum dolor sit amet, consectetur adipisicing elit, sed do eiusmod tempor incididunt ut labore et dolore magna aliqua. Ut enim ad minim veniam, quis nostrud exercitation ullamco*

laboris nisi ut aliquip ex ea commodo consequat. Duis aute irure dolor in reprehenderit in voluptate velit esse cillum dolore eu fugiat nulla pariatur. Excepteur sint occaecat cupidatat non proident, sunt in culpa qui officia deserunt mollit anim id est laborum.

OTHER WORD ODDITIES

An excellent web site dealing with word oddities and trivia is at

http://members.aol.com/gulfhigh2/words.html

It includes lists dealing with interesting aspects such as the following:

- palindromes
- words with uncommon multiple letters
- typewriter words
- words with multiple consecutive consonants
- words commonly misspelt
- pangrams (sentences containing all the letters of the alphabet)
- particularly long words
- names of people which became words.

PART III

LIGHT RELIEF

CHAPTER 14

A Letter From Gloria

If you can't explain it simply, you don't understand it well enough

- Albert Einstein

BACKGROUND

This is an adaptation of an item which first appeared in the Games Magazine *in 1984.*

THE LETTER

Gloria knew what she wanted in life, but like many people she thought punctuation was unimportant. So she sent a simple letter to her John:

> *Dear John I want a man who knows what love is all about you are generous kind thoughtful people who are not like you admit to being useless and inferior you have ruined me for other men I yearn for you I have no feelings whatsoever when we're apart I can be forever happy will you let me be yours Gloria*

What she meant to convey was as follows:

Dear John

I want a man who knows what love is all about. You are generous, kind, thoughtful. People who are not like you admit to being useless and inferior. You have ruined me for other men. I yearn for you. I have no feelings whatsoever when we're apart. I can be forever happy - will you let me be yours?

Gloria

Unfortunately for her, John interpreted the letter rather differently. He thought that it said the following:

Dear John

I want a man who knows what love is. All about you are generous, kind, thoughtful people, who are not like you. Admit to being useless and inferior. You have ruined me. For other men, I yearn. For you, I have no feelings whatsoever. When we're apart, I can be forever happy. Will you let me be?

Yours

Gloria

CHAPTER 15

A Love Letter

Proper words in proper places make
the true definition of style

-Jonathan Swift in
Letter to a young Clergyman

BACKGROUND

This is a love letter from a boy to a girl. However, the girl's father did not like him and wanted them to stop their relationship. The boy thus wrote a short letter to the girl in the terms which follow.

THE LETTER

The great love that I have for you is gone, and I find my dislike for you grows every day. When I see you, I do not even like your face; the one thing that I want to do is to look at other girls. I never wanted to marry you. Our last conversation was very boring and has not made me look forward to seeing you again. You think only of yourself. If we were married, I know that I would find

12 life very difficult, and I would have no
13 pleasure in living with you. I have a heart
14 to give, but it is not something that
15 I want to give to you. No one is more
16 foolish and selfish than you, and you are not
17 able to care for me and help me.
18 I sincerely want you to understand that
19 I speak the truth. You will do me a favor
20 if you think this is the end. Do not try
21 to answer this. Your letters are full of
22 things that do not interest me. You have no
23 true love for me. Good-bye! Believe me,
24 I do not care for you. Please do not think that
25 I am still your boyfriend.

FINALE

However, the boy had previously told the girl to read only the odd-numbered lines.

CHAPTER 16

Fun And Games In The Centre

Dictionary: A malevolent literary device
for cramping the growth of a language
and making it hard and inelastic

- Ambrose Bierce, in
his *Devil's Dictionary*

BACKGROUND

Good writing requires more than just attention to technical aspects such as spelling, grammar and punctuation. A practical example may assist. Reproduced below is a short story which uses humour to convey a quite serious message. It is an edited version of an article by the author which was first published in the Good Weekend *of 27 February 1993.*

THE STORY

The 59th annual general meeting of the Ayers Rock Marbles Club was in session. Old Colonel Twittering was again in the chair, as he had been for the last 35 years. He knew nothing about meetings procedure and little about running sporting competitions, but he was rich and generous with donations and that made him an ideal club president.

In his younger days his name and title had also lent some credibility to the movement and this had been good for recruiting new members. Nowadays, however, his main connection with the sport seemed to be that he had actually lost his marbles.

Club meetings were usually fairly formal but boring events. On this occasion the club had young Miss Joan Fewster sitting next to the colonel in her capacity as acting secretary. Things immediately got off to a poor start. As soon as the apologies had been accepted she rose to her feet and astonished everyone by solemnly proposing her very first motion:

"As the former Secretary has left the district and as the former Minutes cannot be located I now move that the Minutes of the last Annual General Meeting be adopted as they would have been read, had they been found."

Mr Bob Jones attempted to take a point of order at this juncture, but the colonel was a no nonsense man. His idea of good annual meeting was one which was over after about six minutes.

"You can't take a point of order," he ruled in a solemn tone. "It's not on the agenda."

The correspondence included a very nice letter from Bill Smith, the club umpire, who was in hospital recovering from a minor operation. He wrote thanking the president for his recent bedside visit. The president reported that Bill had indeed looked very fit. "He even smiled when I explained that I was there on behalf of the entire committee. I told him that by a vote of 7 to 5 they had resolved to wish him a speedy recovery."

More serious difficulties arose later on in the proceedings. The meeting had before it a proposal to build a magnificent new clubhouse and convention centre for about $2 million.

The trouble was that nobody knew whether this was good value - should the cost really have been $1 million or $3 million? Those present were not willing to show their ignorance and so the motion was passed without debate in about 30 seconds flat.

As luck would have it, the very next item on the agenda was a proposal to send a small gift to the recently retired secretary in recognition of her hard work over the years and as a memento from all her friends. The suggestion was that this should be a book, costing about $20, suitably inscribed by the colonel as president.

All hell let loose. By this time everyone was feeling dreadfully guilty about having passed the previous resolution so quickly. People who could not comment meaningfully on the design of a new major building at least knew what a book was. They could also readily identify with the subject matter of the current motion.

So, in order to demonstrate how responsibly they all took the decision-making process, they debated at length as to which book the club should get, how much it should cost, what precisely the inscription should say, and so on.

After 90 minutes of this an amendment was proposed and carried enthusiastically - it instructed the acting secretary to get further background information and it also appointed a sub-committee to research the whole project in much greater detail!

Actually, this was a dangerous move. Last year a special sub-committee had been requested to choose between two conflicting alternatives and all that they had managed to do was to narrow the choice down to some eight different possibilities.

Shortly afterwards there was a sudden interruption. An excited member burst into the meeting room and shouted loudly: “Mr President, I have an important message from the police. A live bomb has just been found under the clubhouse. I move that it be disposed of immediately.”

Pandemonium broke out as members attempted to take points of order all over the place. Some people asserted that the motion could not be put because 21 days’ notice of it had not been given as required under the rules and others that it had not been validly proposed because the mover had not been given the call.

Others again were concerned because the motion had not been seconded properly. Somebody even tried to move the suspension of standing orders to deal with the matter.

Debate continued fiercely for another 10 minutes ...

BANG!!!

And serve them all jolly well right.

CHAPTER 17

A Modern Fable

A synonym is a word one uses when one cannot spell the right word and therefore cannot find it in the dictionary

\- anon

BACKGROUND

As mentioned in the previous chapter, good writing requires more than just accurate spelling, grammar and punctuation. A further practical example may assist. Reproduced below is another short story by the present author which uses humour to convey some important messages. An earlier version of it was originally included in his book Company Directors: Masters or Servants? *published in 1994.*

THE STORY

Mary Black was a young journalist on the staff of a major metropolitan newspaper. She was not long out of university and her early career had been on the paper's general pages.

However, recently she had been transferred to the business section in order to broaden her experience and this had exposed her to a whole new set of interesting challenges.

Many companies listed on the stock exchange hold press conferences when they release their annual reports. Often company spokesmen are also willing on request to give more detailed background briefings to finance reporters at that time of the year.

Thus it came about that Mary was sent to interview a gentleman whom we will just call John Smith in order to protect the guilty.

Smith was the head of a large public company which for some months had frequently made the headlines on the business pages for its enormous losses and other problems. Its latest result, released a few weeks ago, had been even more dismal than the market had expected.

As it was the reporter's first assignment of this type she was understandably more than a little nervous. However, when she rang the company somewhat to her surprise she got an appointment without difficulty. She thus felt that this would be a relatively easy interview. Perhaps she could even get a human interest angle.

She obtained copies of the company's published annual reports for the last few years and did some homework in anticipation.

Fortuitously, her reporter's notebook subsequently fell off the back of a truck. From this it has now proved possible to reconstruct the conversation which must have taken place and which is reproduced below.

Apparently, when Mary got there Smith welcomed her cordially and she relaxed. After some preliminary chit-chat she got down to the business at hand.

She decided to quote from the company's latest annual report, a thick document which had been sent to all shareholders a few days earlier. She was trying to use this as a convenient opening gambit in order to get her host talking:

"I see that unlike many other organisations your company does not set out its corporate objectives in this document. In practical terms, what are your aims for the next year or two?"

"Are you making any charges?" was Smith's unexpected, angry and irrelevant response. The Great Man, as his subordinates regarded him, had suddenly turned hostile.

"Not at all - I merely wished to know, just what do all these high-sounding words really mean?" she said meekly.

"They mean that we will be increasing the value of our shareholders' investment," he said in a firm voice designed to disguise the uselessness of such a motherhood statement.

"What changes will your group actually be making?"

"Look here, I have in my hand an expert report which we specially commissioned at great expense. Let me read you an extract:

"'Your business plan needs to be a flexible arrangement, put together by a company's management in order to impress lenders and regulatory authorities, and possibly enhanced by carefully worded references to modern digital technology, established games theory, tested interpersonal relationships, stochastic work profiles, time phase communications tools, random economic activities, reciprocal mission statements, purposeful dynamic options, well designed locational incremental functions, third generation style issues, major logistic programs, statistical engineering concepts, prime operational hardware, stable supervisory strategies and the like.'

"There, now are you satisfied?"

"But what does all that this really mean?" she pleaded.

"How dare you question that!" he thundered. "I have just read you part of a letter from a leading international firm of chartered accountants, a team of the highest standing. In fact, this report was prepared by a partner who has held high office in one of the national accountancy bodies. How can you possibly query such expertise?"

"Then how do you explain your recent losses?"

"The weather." He seemed to have a straight face.

"The weather?"

"And we had trouble with several trade unions."

"What sort of trouble?"

"And the Government acted unpredictably."

"Please go on."

"Then some of our computers played up."

"Well?"

"And our competitors increased their market share."

"But ..."

"We lost some important licences."

"So?"

"Our customers just weren't very loyal. The consumer lobbies were on our back. Our auditor was being extremely difficult. Our lawyers kept giving us the wrong advice."

"What exactly are you getting at?" she challenged.

Smith just went on and on, ignoring her again: "Also, the banks let us down. So, you can see that the losses weren't really our fault at all. We are not like our chief competitor, who appointed an expert to advise it on the basis of his prolific ability to produce an infinite variety of incomprehensible figures calculated with micrometric precision from the vaguest of assumptions based on debatable evidence from inconclusive data derived by persons of questionable reliability for the sole purpose of confusing a highly paid but already hopelessly befuddled board of directors who never read the statistics anyway."

She decided to change tack. "Your chairman's address to the company's last annual general meeting was remarkable in that it did not seem to mention your company or its activities even once."

"That is quite right."

"That is quite right?"

"Yes. Actually, it wasn't the official speech we had prepared for him. He had somehow managed to pick up the wrong piece of paper. He just read out a different speech without noticing. After all, he is 87 years old."

"Then why on earth did you not try to stop him?"

"Well, it was quite a good speech anyway - and he has been our chairman for 45 years. He succeeded his father and grandfather. Two of his sons are on our current board. He is such a nice chap. You have to make allowances."

She sighed inwardly and tried a different approach. "In last year's annual report your review of the year mentioned some problems with one of your associated companies. What precisely is the current position?"

"Regrettably, that company is now in liquidation and we have unfortunately lost a lot of money. The company's former chief executive officer is facing serious criminal charges in three States and extradition to New Zealand. He has been accused of putting millions of dollars of public shareholder funds into his private pocket, where they just disappeared. He has also been declared bankrupt. But we expect to get some money back from him."

"Really?" she asked, incredulously. "Just how?"

"Well, he is a very good public speaker, very inspirational, much in demand on the professional lecture circuit. He is beloved by his audiences and he can thus charge very high fees for his frequent appearances at very expensive corporate management seminars."

"What exactly does he speak on?"

"Oh, his most popular topic is 'How to run a business ethically'."

CHAPTER 18

How I Met My Wife

If you have an important point to make,
don't try to be subtle or clever. Use a
pile driver. Hit the point once. Then
come back and hit it again. Then hit it
a third time, a tremendous whack.

- Winston Churchill

BACKGROUND

This fascinating article by Jack Winter was first published in the New Yorker *on 25 July 1994.*

THE STORY

It had been a rough day, so when I walked into the party I was very chalant, despite my efforts to appear gruntled and consolate.

I was furling my wieldy umbrella for the coat check when I saw her standing alone in a corner. She was a descript person, a woman in a state of total array. Her hair was kempt, her clothing shevelled, and she moved in a gainly way.

I wanted desperately to meet her, but I knew I'd have to make bones about it since I was travelling cognito. Beknownst to me, the hostess, whom I could see both hide and hair of, was very proper, so it would be skin off my nose if anything bad happened. And even though I had only swerving loyalty to her, my manners couldn't be peccable. Only toward and heard-of behavior would do.

Fortunately, the embarrassment that my maculate appearance might cause was evitable. There were two ways about it, but the chances that someone as flappable as I would be ept enough to become persona grata or a sung hero were slim. I was, after all, something to sneeze at, someone you could easily hold a candle to, someone who usually aroused bridled passion.

So I decided not to risk it. But then, all at once, for some apparent reason, she looked in my direction and smiled in a way that I could make heads and tails of. I was plussed. It was concerting to see that she was communicado, and it nerved me that she was interested in a pareil like me, sight seen. Normally, I had a domitable spirit, but, being corrigible, I felt capacitated, as if this were something I was great shakes at, and forgot that I had succeeded in situations like this only a told number of times. So, after a terminable delay, I acted with mitigated gall and made my way through the ruly crowd with strong givings.

Nevertheless, since this was all new hat to me and I had no time to prepare a promptu speech, I was petuous. Wanting to make only called-for remarks, I started talking about the hors d'oeuvres, trying to abuse her of the notion that I was sipid, and perhaps even bunk a few myths about myself.

She responded well, and I was mayed that she considered me a savory character who was up to some good. She told me who she was. "What a perfect nomer," I said advertently. The conversation became more and more choate, and we spoke at length to much avail. But I was defatigable, so I had to leave at a godly hour. I asked if she wanted to come with me. To my delight, she was committal. We left the party together and have been together ever since. I have given her my love, and she has requited it.

APPENDIX

Style Manuals - Masters Or Servants?

Paper by the Author to the Style Council in Melbourne, 16 October 2005

To paraphrase the theologian Alexander Campbell (1788-1866), a good motto for all writers might well be:

> *In matters of fact, accuracy; in matters of style, consistency; in all things, clarity.*

WHAT IS A STYLE MANUAL?

The label "style manual" can mean different things to different people, but the broad concept is that such a work should act as an authoritative reference tool for writers, editors, publishers, indexers, printers, designers and web site creators in regard to grammar, spelling, punctuation and word usage.

Other aspects which might be covered could include style issues for which there is no "right" or "wrong", such as rules governing capitalisation, italics, acronyms, date formats and the use of British versus American spelling and gender neutral language. The treatment of quotations, spacing, sub-headings, tables, illustrations, footnotes, references, indices and so on could also be covered. A good manual would also include plenty of examples.

Of course, in some areas there is indeed a "right" or "wrong" approach - for example, metric symbols should be written only in the way specified in an international standard.

A modern style manual also needs to take into consideration that in this age of computers and the Internet not all writing is intended for the printed page.

DESCRIPTIVE VERSUS PRESCRIPTIVE?

Most dictionaries are *descriptive* rather than *prescriptive.* In other words, they summarise alternative current usages but refrain from making value judgements.

However, in order to be useful a style manual really needs to be prescriptive - otherwise one of its key objectives, the encouragement of consistency, would be lost. Furthermore, merely counting heads does nothing to raise standards.

Of course, this does not mean that the users of a particular work cannot depart from its recommendations and substitute their own preferences at will. Rather it means that when they do this it should ideally be as the result of a conscious and reasoned decision on their part.

Inevitably, the authors of prescriptive guides tend to be both passionate and opinionated. Thus their considered views on some issues may well deliberately differ from those of other experts - thus leading not only to intellectual arguments between experts but also to confusion for users. No style manual is meant to have the force of an Act of Parliament.

OFFICIAL GUIDANCE

There is, of course, no official custodian of the English language corresponding to, say, the forty "immortals" comprising the French Academy, who are able to give rulings as to what is acceptable French. The test of what is and what is not good English must thus remain quite subjective.

A popular style manual in this country is the one formerly published by the Australian Government Publishing Service and now published by John Wiley and Sons Australia, Ltd. Originally produced by the Commonwealth Government for the guidance of its own public servants it is now widely used by the private sector and by State Government entities. It, along with *Fowler's Modern English Usage*, can be regarded as de facto official authorities.

Some writers and editors regard such manuals merely as convenient guides to help the attainment of internal consistency in documents and as useful tools helping to raise standards in regard to the four key issues mentioned above - grammar, spelling, punctuation and word usage.

Such persons regard themselves as masters of the situation, able to make decisions in this area and to give expression to their own taste.

Other persons prefer to be slaves, virtually regarding such works as holy writ or messages carved in stone tablets received from up high, to be followed to the letter - forgetting that at best a style manual does no more than reflect the considered personal views, preferences, tastes and biases of its authors and the extent or otherwise of their conservatism and pedantry.

BUSINESSES

In the commercial world few companies other than book and journal publishers have a house style manual of their own. Most have never even thought about the subject and are not familiar with the concept.

A small number of organisations use the AGPS volume "as is". Some supplement it with a house style guide, which can range in size from a single sheet to 50 or more pages. Such guides usually deal with aspects specific to the organisation concerned, such as the style to be used when quoting corporate names and logos or products with registered trade marks. Other aspects covered might relate to technical terms used in particular industries. There might also be a number of overriding rules based on the individual taste of the head of the enterprise concerned.

Business houses are not interested in producing great literature, but they do create communications intended to be read and understood by customers. Their style manuals thus need to cover topics such as layout and the use of jargon, acronyms, political correctness and plain English drafting. Committee productions need rules aimed at achieving internal consistency.

Of course, a house style manual can also deal with certain associated legal issues which, while not really matters of style, may be of particular relevance to an organisation that publishes certain categories of written material. Thus, for example, a discussion of breach of copyright, defamation, contempt of court and contempt of Parliament might be included.

As part of the research for this paper e-mails were sent to a representative sample of 21 companies most but not all of which were listed on the Australian Stock Exchange. They covered a range of sizes and industries, but the sample deliberately excluded companies involved with publishing books, magazines or newspapers.

The recipients were invited to send copies of any style manuals that were being used by their organisations and/or their related companies. The results were rather disappointing. Three companies explicitly stated that they did not use style manuals. The 18 others, by not replying at all, implicitly said the same thing.

The quality of many Australian business letters leaves a lot to be desired. Even publications produced in large numbers - where clearly a certain amount of effort would be justified on economic grounds - are often very poorly written. For example, a few years ago a leading bank sent its millions of customers a letter containing the following sentence: "To remind you of another

Tax, this time being introduced by the Federal Government, is the Federal Bank Account Debits Tax."

Clearly many management teams do not regard the use of good English in their organisations as important. Only on rare occasions do they arrange for their staffs to receive appropriate training, to counter the weaknesses in the education system.

TAKEOVERS

Companies sometimes acquire subsidiaries in takeovers and then rationalise staff and facilities. However, unifying word styles would be well down their list of priorities. The correct or elegant use of the English language would not be regarded as a profit centre.

Quite apart from inertia or ignorance, such companies might also want to retain as much of the separate cultures of their newly acquired subsidiaries as possible, so as not to needlessly upset employees or customers.

OVERSEAS OWNED COMPANIES

Some overseas based companies operate in Australia through subsidiaries. The extent of control from head office would vary according to the circumstances, but usually the Australian offshoots would be allowed freedom to run their affairs to fit in with local conditions - regulatory legislation, taxation, labour conditions, markets and so on are all going to be different in different countries. There is also the tyranny of distance.

A German parent would not expect its Australian subsidiaries to communicate with their own customers other than in the local language, and the same principle would also hold for US parents. The imposition of overseas style on local offshoots would make little sense.

As indicated above most companies operating in Australia do not even have a style manual of their own. Their overseas parents would in any case be more concerned with issues affecting group profitability, such as the effective use of capital and the choice of markets and products. Questions of style would be regarded as quite unimportant administrative details.

If a manual developed in Australia were regarded as suitable for use in, say, the United States then, having regard to the extreme parochialism prevalent in that country, the most likely approach would be to produce an American version for use in that country rather than to force US style onto Australian customers.

PUBLISHERS

In contrast to other organisations, companies involved with publishing books, newspapers and magazines usually do have quite elaborate style manuals and seek to enforce their use on their own writers and editors. These manuals are nowadays stored electronically on computers and made readily accessible on an intranet. Such a format also makes it easy to keep the guidance up-to-date.

However, such efforts are not always successful - possibly because a very large manual gets put into the mental "too hard" basket instead of being read and followed. Furthermore, too much detail supplied to outside authors can thus be counterproductive.

In newspapers and other multi-author publications consistency of style becomes important - particularly in regard to aspects such as hyphens and capitals, where any rules tend to be arbitrary.

However, in the case of self-contained books by a single author strict adherence to a publisher's house style makes less sense, as long as the author has a logical style guide of his or her own and achieves internal consistency.

Typically, the instructions to authors are to the effect "this is how we do it", without any implied claim to be following some universal standard.

A worrying aspect arises where insistence on exact conformity to a journal's house style becomes a determinant when considering the publication of a submitted manuscript.

INFORMAL APPROACHES

There are also less formal style guides for certain common situations - although these are usually not given grandiose titles. To illustrate:

- Public relations organisations issue lists of words and phrases which are regarded as being particularly effective and desirable in public utterances, as well as lists of terms to be avoided because of their negative connotations.
- In the medical world doctors and nurses are given instructions that prescribe the form in which hospital medical notes are to be completed.
- Schools issue edicts on how students' reports are to be completed by their teachers and setting out features such as the denigration of students which are to be avoided.
- Church authorities make suggestions to their clergy in regard to the form of words to be used (or not used) on certain issues when speaking from the pulpit or when writing for church publications.
- The news scripts of commercial television channels follow a special genre which has regard to the time constraints and the visual nature of the medium.

SPECIALIST GUIDES

Although perhaps not widely known to professional linguists, some fairly elaborate published guides can also be found in certain specialist situations.

Three very different examples will illustrate this point:

- In 1987 the (former) Law Reform Commission of Victoria produced an 80-page publication: *Plain English and the Law: Guidelines for Drafting in Plain English: A Manual for Legislative Drafters.* It discusses at length topics such as the importance of organisation in Acts of Parliament and aspects of legal vocabulary. However, many of the principles would also apply to commercial contracts, to reports and to formal submissions.
- The Melbourne PC User Group Inc. has published on its web site an 11-page *Style Guide for Authors and Sub-editors: How to Prepare Submissions for Publication*, specifically for contributors to its own monthly journal *PC Update* - although no doubt this well thought-out summary would be equally helpful to other writers in this area. As one would expect, it sets out inter alia a detailed standard for rendering many common computer-related terms and symbols.
- Deakin University has produced a *Chemistry Style Manual* of over 200 pages to assist its students. It, too, is available online.

UNITED STATES

Unlike Australia the United States does not have a single widely used style manual. Instead, the guidance is fragmented over works such as the *Chicago Manual of Style*, the *Associated Press Stylebook*, the *Gregg Reference Manual* and *Words Into Type*.

For scientific and similar publications the *APA Publication Manual* produced by the American Psychological Association is favoured, while the *MLA Style Manual* produced by the Modern Language Association is often used for works involving the humanities.

As in Australia, there are also a number of specialist manuals, such as those designed for writers in the fields of science, medicine or the humanities.

To make matters worse, different editions of some of the four standard works mentioned above appear to be in concurrent use. Thus users looking for authoritative "holy writ" guidance instead often encounter quasi-theological disputes!

Some persons who have been trained to use a particular manual are quite lost if they cannot find an answer to something bothering them. Because of such brainwashing they even become too frightened to use their discretion.

A LACK OF LOGIC

Another problem is that some of the advice given in these works is quite idiotic, thus rather detracting from their credibility. Consider the following sentence:

> *Authors seem to be avoiding "must".*

Australian and British writers would render such a sentence as above, with the full stop logically following the closing quotation marks.

However, most American writers slavishly following their style manuals would instead write:

> *Authors seem to be avoiding "must."*

Putting the full stop before the closing quotation marks in this type of sentence does not make sense, yet this formula is actually *prescribed* for full stops and commas - although strangely enough the reverse is prescribed for semi-colons and colons. Americans seem unconcerned at this curious inconsistency.

The Australian punctuation also works if more than one quoted term is involved - for example:

> *Authors seem to be avoiding both "must" and "shall".*

Of course, there are contexts where quotation mark needs to follow the stop - for example:

> *"Come here," she said.*

The illogical style discussed above is apparently taught in American schools. This reflects badly on the education system in the United States. American writers seem unconcerned because they are used to it - it is regarded as traditional in the good old USA.

The idiotic American punctuation mentioned above is akin to the absurd American system of writing dates (namely, month-day-year instead of either day-month-year or year-month-day). To non-American this sort of thing makes the United States look an astonishingly backward country.

While a few adventurous Americans are now using logical full stops and commas, the linguistic fundamentalists persist in defending the indefensible.

American copy editors who still slavishly follow one or other of the American style manuals mentioned above should throw away their chains and disregard nonsensical rulings even if they appear in such works. They should wean away any publishers who expect these to be followed. They should start punctuating in a way that is not only logical but also in universal use throughout the rest of the world.

INTERNATIONAL ASPECTS

Unfortunately, by now the possibility of having a single style manual usable in Australia, Britain and the United States must be regarded as a lost cause.

Naturally, this causes great difficulties for authors and publishers who wish to cater for these three important markets (as well as those in other English-speaking countries).

Foisting Australian spelling and expressions onto American customers would greatly prejudice sales and even bookstore acceptance. Producing two separate editions would be an expensive solution, not feasible except for best-sellers. The most economic solution would probably be to produce only an

American version - while this might annoy Australian readers it would be unlikely to stop their purchases of the work.

Generally speaking, none of the three versions of English can be regarded as “right” or “wrong” in any absolute sense - various versions are just *different* - although naturally there are some exceptions to this proposition, such as the one involving quotation marks which was discussed above.

CONCLUSION

Questions of morality or legality simply do not come into any meaningful discussion of English language style issues; the so-called “rules” are merely a matter of taste and tradition, in much the same way as in the case of dress codes.

Glossary

101: comprising the introductory material in, or as if in, a formal course of study - for example, "English Grammar 101".

angle: the particular approach used in a piece of writing.

Anton Pillar order: a legally binding court order which allows an applicant, without prior notice to the respondent, to enter the respondent's premises and to inspect and/or seize documents or other items. It is designed to prevent the destruction of incriminating evidence - for example, in connection with the alleged illegal use of copyrighted software or other material.

baby boomers: the generation of persons in Western countries born between the end of World War II in 1945 and about 1965. This generation is much larger than the preceding and following generations. At the time of their young adulthood its members saw massive changes in attitudes to many social issues, including opposition to the Vietnam War, the sexual revolution and mass political action for causes such as civil rights and feminism. See also generation X.

BAPH: Brisbane, Adelaide, Perth and Hobart.

BAPH States: the Australian States other than Victoria and New South Wales.

billion, trillion: originally a billion was a million million and a trillion was a million million million - a coherent pattern. Unfortunately, a different, quite illogical, usage developed in the

United States and France and has now taken over. Under this approach, a billion is 1000 million and a trillion is 1000 billion.

boiler plate clauses: standardised text, usable as a template in letters, contracts, annual reports and so on.

breach of confidence: the disclosure of information to a person not entitled to it by someone who has an obligation to keep it confidential.

business plan: a document which describes a company's management, business concepts and corporate objectives (both short term and long term). It is a vital tool for any company seeking bank loans or any other type of outside investment funding, but it can also be of great value in clarifying the realities for the owners of the enterprise themselves. A business plan should include details of the finance being injected by the proprietors and the expected internal rate of return; an assessment of the target market and the likely competition; a summary of the board and management team and their experience and expertise; brief job descriptions for the key employees and a summary of their contractual arrangements; balance sheet, profit and loss and cash flow projections; the attractions of the product or service for potential customers; details of the premises to be used and of any leases; marketing plans; any proposed Internet presence; and so on (as appropriate to the particular case).

byline: the name of the author of an article, set out at its beginning.

convergence (physical equipment): the trend for television, telephones and computers to become a single instrument, as all content is converging into digital streams of information that can represent text, graphics, audio or video, and can be distributed over multiple media such as satellites, CDs, DVDs, cable lines, wireless and land-based telephone connections.

copyright: the exclusive but marketable right to publish and distribute original literary, artistic and similar works. Copyright automatically belongs initially to the creator of a work and lasts for his or her lifetime and for a further 50 years. The rights can be assigned to other persons in whole or in part. Many authors grant licences in exchange for royalties.

cyberspace: everything on the Internet.

data mining: the analysis of large groups of data in a database, using tools which look for previously unknown trends or anomalies or hidden patterns, without regard to the meaning of the data.

FAQ: a list of "frequently asked questions" and their answers. Such lists are a popular feature of the Internet, but the concept can be used in other contexts.

generation X: the generation of persons born in Western countries during the period from the early 1960s to the late 1970s - persons widely regarded as being disillusioned, cynical and apathetic. See also baby boomers.

generation Y: the generation of persons following generation X, usually taken as persons born in Western countries during the period from the late 1970s to the turn of the century.

ghostwriter: a person who by arrangement writes something which purports to have been written by another person, usually someone well-known but lacking the time or ability to carry out the task personally.

grammar slack: the tolerance exhibited by most Internet users for small spelling and grammatical errors.

home page: an organisation's main page on a World Wide Web site.

house style manual: a reference work for use by those on a company's staff charged with putting words together, helping these to raise the standard of their spelling, grammar and punctuation and also to ensure internal consistency throughout the company's publications. The manual can be a printed guide to matters of style or it can be set up on a computer accessible to staff and updated as required.

ibid: (in citations of books, etc.) in the same place.

intellectual property (IP): intangible assets derived from original thought and protected by law - ideas, discoveries and inventions. The protection comes about from laws covering patents, copyright (literature, music, art, software and so on) and trademarks.

Internet: a co-operative public network of shared information stored on computers. See also Appendices A and D.

International Standard Book Number (ISBN): a unique 10-digit code for the identification of printed books and pamphlets and various other material (but not serial publications - see next item).

International Standard Serial Number (ISSN): a unique 8-digit code for the identification of serial publications, including periodical newsletters produced by organisations.

inverted pyramid: an article in which the most important information is written first and the least important last.

Keynesian economics: the advocacy of monetary and fiscal programs by governments in order to increase employment and spending and to stimulate business activity. This economic theory was originally put forward by John Maynard Keynes in his book *The General Theory of Employment, Interest and Money* (1936). Keynes was of the view that high employment and controlled inflation could best be achieved by the authorities varying interest rates, tax rates and public expenditures rather than relying on market forces.

lead: the opening paragraph in a story published in the media or in a media release.

legal deposit: the statutory requirement for all publishers in Australia to deposit free of charge on its issue one copy of each of their publications with the appropriate State Library and also with the National Library of Australia in Canberra. These provisions apply to both commercial and non-commercial publishing activities.

media release: a written communication setting out a statement which is intended for publication as a news story in newspapers and/or on radio and television.

netizen: a person who uses the Internet frequently.

normal distribution (statistics): a distribution of scores around an expected value where variations are caused by random factors. When plotted, the scores form a symmetrical bell-shaped curve.

Pareto principle: the "80-20 rule", which states that for many phenomena 80 per cent of the consequences stem from 20 per cent of the causes - for example, that 80 per cent of wealth is owned by 20 per cent of the population, or that 80 per cent of turnover comes from 20 per cent of customers.

passim: (in a quoted work) in various places.

preamble: words at the beginning of a submission or similar document which give some background to it or set it in context.

resolution: a formal determination by an organised meeting.

search engine: a computer program and an associated database maintained on a special Internet site which in combination enable any Internet user to make keyword searches for desired information. The database performs a similar function to a library catalogue and is in effect a very large index of web pages derived from the electronic inspection of a great number of individual sites according to rules which are similar in character but different in detail for each search engine.

sound bite: a brief segment of remarks by some spokesperson recorded and on radio or television.

submission: a document commenting on social issues or seeking some political objective, such as might be made to a government or to an official inquiry, especially a document setting out relevant facts, opinions, arguments, analyses, statistical data and/or recommendations for action, or soliciting funding for some worthwhile purpose.

verbatim: exactly as spoken.

World Wide Web (WWW or "web"): the Internet information retrieval system which originated from the CERN high energy physics laboratories in Geneva, Switzerland. The information on WWW pages is usually represented using the HyperText Markup Language (HTML) (see above), enabling computer users everywhere, when connected to the Internet, to obtain ready access to other web documents. A special program, known as a "browser" (see above), is employed by users for this purpose.

Tailpiece

Samuel Johnson, the famous lexicographer, was once caught by his wife cuddling the maid.

She exclaimed: “Samuel, I am surprised!”

“No, my dear,” he responded, “it is I who am surprised. As for you, you are astonished.”

* * *

Having committed political suicide, the Conservative Party is now living to regret it. - Chris Patten

* * *

A famous linguist, visiting Ireland, asked an Irish colleague, whether the Irish language had a word meaning the same as the Spanish “manana”.

“Sure,” said the Irishman, “we have two or three that come close. But none of them has quite the same sense of urgency.”

* * *

Irony in high places: What should one do with an ABC presenter who refers to that organisation’s Standing Committee on Spoken English as the “SCOSE *committee*”?

* * *

Six per cent of the population can’t read. The other 90 per cent can’t do arithmetic.

* * *

A Freudian slip is when you say one thing but mean your mother.

* * *

Diner in restaurant: These eggs aren't fresh.

Waitress: Don't blame me. I only laid the table.

* * *

Girl, to amorous boy-friend: Go easy, I'm virgo intacta.

Boy: Oh, I can speak Latin, too. I'm infra dig.

* * *

One day a graffiti writer put a political slogan in regard to the Prime Minister on a wall. Over the next few days several other graffiti writers came along and made slight additions to the message. The five versions read as follows:

HOWARD

OUT HOWARD

SHOUT HOWARD

SHOUT DOWN WITH HOWARD

SHOUT DOWN WITH HOWARD'S ENEMIES

* * *

It isn't pollution that's harming the environment; it's the impurities in our air and water that are doing it. - Al Gore

* * *

A recent survey found that 65 per cent of high school students did not know how to use a thesaurus.

A spokesman for the publisher of Roget's Thesaurus said that he found this result "disappointing, unsatisfactory, discouraging and distressing".

* * *

Found in a dictionary:

Circular Definition: see Definition, Circular.

Definition, Circular: see Circular Definition.

* * *

In the course of an essay a student defined "convent" as a place where nuns are confined.

His teacher wrote in the margin that this was obviously either a misconception or a clerical error.

* * *

"Have you a pen?" he asked. "I need to make a mental note."

* * *

Is an electric shaver cutting edge technology?

* * *

Sign on a bus stop: "Route 200: Pick up and set down only."

As distinct from other bus stops?

* * *

He taught himself to read by taking a correspondence course.

* * *

Sometimes the last four words of something do matter.

An entertainer on stage held up a large placard reading "ABCDEF" and asked his assistant to read it out aloud to the audience.

The assistant read out "ABCDEK".

The exasperated entertainer then chided him: "Every time I show you F you see K."

* * *

Does the name "Pavlov" ring a bell?

* * *

Newsreader: Early today the senator called a spade a spade. Later on he issued a retraction.

* * *

I have made this letter longer than usual, only because I have not had the time to make it shorter. - Blaise Pascal

* * *

Bus driver: When you exit this vehicle, please lower your head and watch your step. If you fail to do so, please lower your voice and watch your language.

* * *

The problem with the French is that they don't have a word for "entrepreneur". - attributed to President George W Bush

* * *

Some persons believe that being able to swear at people in their own language constitutes being multilingual.

* * *

When a customer received a new credit card from his bank, it had the Arabic numeral "3" after his name. He felt that it should instead have had the Roman numeral "III", to indicate that his name was the same as that of his father and grandfather.

So he called the bank's customer service number and asked that their records be changed to fix this.

The customer service representative who answered the telephone was polite but firm. "I'm very sorry, sir," she explained, "but none of our computers has Roman numerals."

* * *

There once was a lady from Crewe

Whose limericks always stopped at line two.

* * *

In the last two-and-a-half hours we've had about five hundred orders ... people obviously want something unique - the vendor of memorabilia which showed a superseded date

* * *

Two actual queries from library users reported by reference desk staffers:

"I need to find out Ibid's first name for my bibliography."

"Why don't you have any books by Ibid? He's written a lot of important stuff."

* * *

In 1921, Chinese ambassador Wellington Koo visited America to represent China at the Washington Conference. At one banquet he found himself seated beside a woman who, after several minutes of embarrassed silence, attempted to begin a conversation: "Likee soupee?" she asked.

Koo merely nodded politely and continued with his meal.

Some time later, he was called upon to deliver the keynote address to the guests - which he did for some 45 minutes in impeccable English.

Sitting down, he turned to his neighbour and asked: "Likee speechee?"

* * *

"Enter your current date of birth" - question on an insurance renewal form.

* * *

Condoms should be used on every conceivable occasion.

* * *

One important fact about Murphy's Law is that it was not actually coined by Murphy, but by another man of the same name.

* * *

A young Australian tourist was enjoying his first night in Rome drinking cappuccino at a pavement cafe when a pretty girl sat down beside him.

"Hello," he said. "Do you understand English?"

"Only a little," she answered.

"How much?" he asked.

"Fifty dollars," she replied.

* * *

The telephone at a large company rang. The person answering it said: "Smith and Jones Limited, this is Mary."

The woman on the other end asked: "Who is that?"

Mary replied: "With whom did you wish to speak, madam?"

There was a long pause and then the woman said: "Did you just say 'whom'?"

Mary: "Yes, I did."

Woman: "Then I must have the wrong number." Click.

* * *

Illiterate? Write in for our free brochure.

* * *

All right, everyone, line up alphabetically according to your height. - Casey Stengel

* * *

If you're not fired with enthusiasm, you'll be fired with enthusiasm. - Vince Lombardi, a coach in the United States to his team members

* * *

Stressing the importance of a large vocabulary, an English teacher told his class, "Use a word ten times and it will be yours for life."

In the back of the room a pert blonde closed her eyes and was heard chanting under her breath: "Fred, Fred, Fred, Fred, Fred, Fred, Fred, Fred, Fred, Fred."

* * *

Copying extensively from one source is plagiarism; copying extensively from several is research. - anon

* * *

Time flies like the wind. Fruit flies like a banana. - Groucho Marx

* * *

I like pigs. Dogs look up to us. Cats look down on us. Pigs treat us as equals. - Winston Churchill

* * *

The longest word is the word that follows the announcement: "And now a word from our sponsor." - Red Skelton

* * *

What is another word for thesaurus?

* * *

Good girls say, "Don't. Stop." Bad girls say, "Don't stop."

* * *

Your food stamps will be stopped effective March 1992, because we received notice that you had passed away. May God bless you. You may reapply if there is a change in your circumstances. - Letter from the Greenville County Department of Social Services

* * *

There is no difference between theory and practice in theory but there is in practice.

* * *

It's deja vu all over again. - Yogi Berra

* * *

A tourist picked up a cab at Boston Airport and asked, "Can you tell me where I can get scrod?"

The cabby replied, "Sure, but I've never heard it expressed in the pluperfect subjunctive before."

* * *

A gentleman, having ordered a meal at a fine London restaurant, decided that he would like some wine to accompany his meal. So he summoned the wine steward and asked for a bottle of hock.

"Hock, sir?" asked the steward.

"Yes, hock, man. You know: hic, hunc, huius, huic, hoc."

"Hmm ... very good, sir."

The food duly arrived, but without the wine. This perturbed the gentleman slightly, as he was accustomed to a higher standard of service. He began to dine, and at the next opportunity he beckoned the steward again.

"Didn't I order a bottle of hock?"

"Yes, sir, you did - but then you declined it."

* * *

A Swiss man, looking for directions, pulled up at a bus stop where two Americans were waiting.

“Entschuldigung, koennen Sie Deutsch sprechen?” he asked. The two Americans just stared at him.

“Excusez-moi, parlez-vous Francais?” he tried. The two continued to stare.

“Parlano l’italiano?” No response.

“Hablan ustedes Espanol?” Still nothing. The Swiss guy drove off, totally frustrated.

The first American turned to the second and said, “Y’know, maybe we should learn a foreign language.”

“Why?” asked the other. “That guy knew four languages, and it didn’t do him any good.”

* * *

Notice in a book: Spelling mistakes have been left in this work for people who need to correct others in order to make their life fulfilled.

* * *

Answering machine: If you want to buy marijuana, press the hash key now.

* * *

A man told his doctor that he wasn’t able to do all the things around the house that he used to do.

When the examination was complete, he said: “Now, Doc, I can take it. Tell me in plain English what’s wrong with me.”

“Well, in plain English,” the doctor replied, “you’re just a very lazy old man.”

“Thank you,” said the man. “Now give me the medical term, so that I can tell my wife.”

* * *

Lady of the house: I want you to stand at the front door and call the guests' names as they arrive.

Butler: Very well, madam. I've been wanting to do that for years.

* * *

A preacher's wife proofread his Sunday sermon and wrote next to one paragraph: "Weak point - shout loudly."

* * *

Samuel Johnson was once sent a manuscript by an aspiring writer.

Johnson replied, "Your manuscript is both good and original, but the part that is good is not original and the part that is original is not good."

* * *

I used to spell and grammar badlie but now I got worser.

* * *

A listed company launched a hostile takeover bid for one of its competitors.

The chairman of the bidding company wrote a letter to the chairman of the target company. It commenced, politely enough: "I want the pleasure of your company."

* * *

If a word is misspelled in a dictionary, how would one ever know?

* * *

Synonym: A word which one can use when one cannot spell the other one.

* * *

The evening news is where they begin with "Good evening" and then proceed to tell you why it isn't. - anon

* * *

Extract from an English Literature student's essay: "Magna Carta provided that no man should be hanged twice for the same offence."

* * *

You are calling me a sceptic? I trust that you have proof.

* * *

Newspapers publish death notices every day. But just how do they manage to get the people to die in alphabetical order?

* * *

If I have a bunch of odds and ends and get rid of all but one of them, what should I call it?

* * *

A journalism student was told that the most popular newspaper stories were those involving religion, royalty, sex and crime, plus a spot of mystery.

Such stories did not need to be very long, it was pointed out - for example: "My God," said the Queen, "I'm pregnant. Who done it?"

* * *

Q: What are the most imaginative works of fiction being written in Australia today?

A: Income tax returns.

* * *

Q: What are the two most beautiful words in the English language?

A: "Cheque enclosed".

* * *

Q: What does "virus" mean?

A: It is a Latin word meaning that your guess is as good as mine.

* * *

Q: What does "vasectomy" mean?

A: It means never having to say that you are sorry.

* * *

Q: What does "zymurgy" mean?

A: I don't know.

Q: I have asked six other people and they all agree with you.

* * *

Q: What does "sarchasm" mean?

A: It is the gulf between the author of sarcastic wit and the recipient who doesn't get it.

* * *

Q: What is the difference between ignorance and apathy?

A: I don't know and I don't care.

* * *

Q: What do you call Santa's Helpers?

A: Subordinate clauses!

* * *

From 1934 to 1939 *Webster's New International Dictionary* included an entry for the word "dord". However, there is no such word in the English language. The error came about because listings were intended for both "D" and "d" as abbreviations of the word "density" and someone misread the notation "D or d" on a card.

* * *

An English professor complained to the pet shop proprietor, "The parrot I purchased from you uses improper language."

"I'm very surprised to hear that," said the owner. "I've never taught that bird to swear."

"Oh, it isn't that," explained the professor. "But yesterday I heard him split an infinitive."

* * *

The manager of a large city zoo was drafting a letter to order a pair of animals. He sat at his computer and typed the following sentence: "I would like to place an order for two mongooses, to be delivered at your earliest convenience."

He stared at the screen, focusing on that odd word "mongooses". Then he deleted the word and added another, so that the sentence now read: "I would like to place an order for two mongeese, to be delivered at your earliest convenience."

Again he stared at the screen, this time focusing on the new word, which seemed just as odd as the original one. So he started once more, this time typing: "I would like to place an order for one mongoose, to be delivered at your earliest convenience." He then added a postscript: "On reflection, make that two."

* * *

An article for the precise cook:

"Adhesion of Rice Flour-Based Batter to Chicken Drumsticks Evaluated by Laser Scanning Confocal Microscopy and Texture Analysis" by A Mukprasirt, T J Herald, D L Boyle and K D Rausch, Poultry Science, vol. 79, no. 9, September 2000, pp. 1356-1363.

* * *

The Archbishop of Canterbury once visited New York. At the airport he was asked by a reporter whether he was going to visit any of the famous naughty night clubs in that city. The

Archbishop smiled sweetly and asked "Where are the naughty night clubs in New York?"

The headline next morning was: "Archbishop's first question on arrival: 'Where are the naughty night clubs in New York?'"

* * *

The publisher of a dictionary went to his lawyer, seeking advice on copyright aspects.

The lawyer advised: "Why don't you put a few deliberate mistakes into your dictionary? Then if somebody copies the text you will have incontrovertible evidence of the infringement."

"Oh," said the publisher, "we don't need to do that. We have quite enough mistakes without trying."

* * *

A judge was interviewing a woman regarding her pending divorce, and asked, "What are the grounds for your divorce?"

She replied, "About four acres and a nice little home in the middle of the property with a stream running by."

"No," he said, "I mean what is the foundation of this case?"

"It is made of concrete, bricks and mortar," she responded.

"I mean," he continued, "what are your relations like?"

"I have an aunt and uncle living here in town, and so do my husband's parents."

He said, "Do you have a real grudge?"

"No," she replied, "we have a two-car carport and have never really needed one."

"Please," he tried again, "is there any infidelity in your marriage?"

"Yes, both my son and daughter have stereo sets. We don't necessarily like the music, but the answer to your question is 'yes'."

"Ma'am, does your husband ever beat you up?"

"Yes," she responded, "about twice a week he gets up earlier than I do."

Finally, in frustration, the judge asked, "Lady, why do you want a divorce?"

"Oh, I don't want a divorce," she replied. "I've never wanted a divorce. My husband does. He says that he can't communicate with me."

* * *

"Now we come to the verbal part of your employment test," said the interviewer. "Can you tell me what 'gross aggrandised annuity' means?"

"Certainly," replied the applicant. "It means that I don't get the job."

* * *

George W Bush was opening the Olympic Games and had to read a speech.

"Oh," he said, "oh, oh, oh, ..."

An aide nudged him gently, "Mr President, please stop," he whispered. "You're reading the Olympic symbol."

* * *

One day in a contract law class, the professor asked one of his better students, "Now, if you were to give someone an orange, how would you go about it?"

The student replied, "I'd say 'Hey, want an orange?'"

The professor was livid. "No! No! Think like a lawyer!" he instructed.

"Oh," the student said. "In that case, I'd tell him, 'I hereby give and convey to you, all and singular, my estate and interests, rights, claim, title and advantages of and in, the said orange, together with all its rind, juice, pulp and seeds, and all rights and advantages with full power to bite, cut, freeze and otherwise eat the same, or give the same away with or without the said rind, juice, pulp and seeds, anything herein before or hereinafter or in any deed or deeds, instruments of whatever nature or kind whatsoever to the contrary in anywise notwithstanding."

"Now you're making good progress," the professor said.

* * *

Some schoolboy howlers from the United States:

- In January, the president makes his Inaugural Address after he has been sworn at.
- Universal suffrage means that even the illegible get to vote.
- Noncommittal is to be able to talk and talk without saying anything.

* * *

A respected church leader arrived in a large city to deliver a series of speeches. At a banquet on the first evening he noticed some reporters in the audience. Because he wanted to use some of the stories he told that night in his speeches the next day, he asked the reporters to omit them from their articles.

This request led to an article the next day containing the line: "Mr Smith also told a number of very good stories that cannot be printed."

* * *

Clancy of the Information Overflow

I'd word-processed him a letter
Which for want of better
Knowledge faxed to where I had a telecon with him just a few hours ago

He was on his Mac when I met him
So I also e-mailed the letter to him
Just on spec, addressed as follows:
Clancy:/o.t.info.oflow.au

And an answer came directed by e-mail unexpected
(And I think the same was done on a laptop while sitting in a car)
'Twas his surfing mate who wrote it and verbatim I will quote it:
Clancy's gone to France Soir lunching but nowadays he's never far.

In my wild erratic fancy visions come to me of Clancy
Gone a'surfing cross the net where the other netheads go
As the web is ever expanding, Clancy's interfacing and flaming
For the surfer's life has pleasure that ordinary folk never know.

And the net hath friends to meet him and their kindly messages greet him
In the murmur of the Mac and the tapping of the space bar
And he sees the vision splendid of virtual realty extended
And at night the wondrous glory of cyberspace without a star.

And I somewhat fancy that I'd like to change with Clancy
Like to take a turn at surfing where the seasons never go
While he faced the world external of the family and diurnal
But I doubt he'd suit this, Clancy:/o.t.info.oflow.au

- Gordon Shaw